Sport, Education and Corporatisation

Using an interdisciplinary approach, *Sport, Education and Corporatisation* offers an important critique of the intersection between sport organisations, commercial agendas and educational development. It reveals a discomforting interplay between sector stakeholders that has been normalised via discourses of civic 'good', social responsibility and community welfare.

The book employs stakeholder theory, corporate social responsibility ideals and holistic constructions of space to provide a framework to understand some of the latent and explicit complexities of sport sector connectivity. Interrogating the key contexts, issues and challenges that emerge from the Sport-Education-Corporate nexus and drawing upon evidence from international, national and local sport organisations, it argues for sustained and rigorous examination of the commercialisation of educational agendas and new directions for education-based corporate social responsibility within the sport industry.

This is an invaluable resource for researchers working in the areas of sport management; sport development; sociology of sport; sport policy and politics; physical education; and the wider economics, organisational politics and business ethics fields. It is also a fascinating read for students within sport business management, sports studies, sport politics and physical education programmes.

Geoffery Z. Kohe is Lecturer in the School of Sport and Exercise Sciences at the University of Kent, UK.

Holly Collison is Lecturer in the Institute of Sport Business at Loughborough University London, UK.

Routledge Focus on Sport, Culture and Society

Routledge Focus on Sport, Culture and Society showcases the latest cutting-edge research in the sociology of sport and exercise. Concise in form (20,000–50,000 words) and published quickly (within three months), the books in this series represents an important channel through which authors can disseminate their research swiftly and make an impact on current debates. We welcome submissions on any topic within the socio-cultural study of sport and exercise, including but not limited to subjects such as gender, race, sexuality, disability, politics, the media, social theory, Olympic Studies, and the ethics and philosophy of sport. The series aims to be theoretically-informed, empirically-grounded and international in reach, and will include a diversity of methodological approaches.

Available in this series:

Christianity and the Transformation of Physical Education and Sport in China
Huijie Zhang, Fan Hong and Fuhua Huang

Skill Transmission, Sport and Tacit Knowledge
A Sociological Perspective
Honorata Jakubowska

Rethinking Sports and Integration
Developing a Transnational Perspective on Migrants and Descendants in Sports
Sine Agergaard

Sport, Education and Corporatisation
Spaces of Connection, Contestation and Creativity
Geoffery Z. Kohe and Holly Collison

For more information: https://www.routledge.com/sport/series/RFSCS

Sport, Education and Corporatisation

Spaces of Connection, Contestation and Creativity

Geoffery Z. Kohe and Holly Collison

Routledge
Taylor & Francis Group

LONDON AND NEW YORK

First published 2019
by Routledge
2 Park Square, Milton Park, Abingdon, Oxon OX14 4RN

and by Routledge
52 Vanderbilt Avenue, New York, NY 10017

First issued in paperback 2020

*Routledge is an imprint of the Taylor & Francis Group, an informa
business*

British Library Cataloguing-in-Publication Data
A catalogue record for this book is available from the British Library

Library of Congress Cataloging-in-Publication Data
A catalog record has been requested for this book

ISBN 13: 978-0-367-67185-3 (pbk)
ISBN 13: 978-0-8153-5601-1 (hbk)

Typeset in Times New Roman by
codeMantra

Contents

Acknowledgements

While this book reflects both of our peripatetic academic genealogies, the genesis of our intellectual partnership and friendship began more recently. In 2015 we were both fortunate to attend a 'Sport & Social Transformation: Sport development and sport mega events' workshop funded by the British Research Council, Newton Fund and Brazilian Federal Research Council (FAPESP) in Sao Paolo, Brazil. Hosted by the University of Bath and University of Sao Paolo, the event brought us into contact with a diverse range of interdisciplinary scholars to critique sport, mega-events and community intersections, and posit new modes of thinking and doing within and across the sport sector. The sentiments of the event, and the challenge to advance interrogations of sport in new ways, have been taken up in this book. As such, we would like to thank Professor Tess Kay and Professor Simone Fullagar for extending us this opportunity. To Tess, thank you also for your warm words of wisdom and motivation, and for nurturing our ideas early on.

We are grateful to the team of reviewers who provided helpful feedback and suggestions on our initial proposal. The extent of feedback on our plans was humbling, and we have endeavoured to engage with the critiques and ideas as much as possible. We certainly feel the book is stronger and has wider appeal as a result.

We would also like to thank the team at Taylor and Francis, in particular Simon Whitmore, Rebecca Connor and Cecily Davey. We were heartened by the positive endorsement you gave, and your encouragement and support through the process has been incredibly useful and much appreciated.

To our colleagues and friends at the University of Loughborough, University of Kent and University of Worcester, and further beyond, we also extend our gratitude. Amid the contextual challenges of academia, your collective ongoing collegiality, intellectual rigour, interest, empathy and generosity of spirit have been genuinely appreciated and needed.

To our respective families, near and far, thank you for your enduring patience, love and support. You created the spaces that made this book.

Geoffery Z. Kohe & Holly Collison
December 2018

1 Interdisciplinary antecedents, contexts and encouragements

Introduction

In many local, regional and global contexts creating and sustaining opportunities for people to play and engage in sport, physical activity and leisure has become increasingly recognised as a matter of concern (Banda & Gultresa, 2015; Coalter, 2010, 2013; Lavalette, 2013; Lindsey et al., 2017; Spaaij, 2012). These debates have been precipitated by an array of factors and forces. These have included, for example, substantive empirical evidence about the need to enhance individuals' and communities' health, wealth, lifestyles and well-being (and productivity), and universal calls to improve related service and industry provision to the public and specialist populations. To these ends, substantive scholarship and public policies have noted the 'transformative' potential and utility of sport/physical education for improving personal development, educational attainment, identity construction, community development, social cohesion, empowerment and emancipation, political agency and cultural awareness (Green, 2009; Green & Smith, 2016; Houlihan, 2016; MacDonald, 2014; Wilson & Hayhurst, 2009; Wright & MacDonald, 2010). Adding to this have been sustained challenges to State, private and third sector financial systems that have altered funding arrangements and fuelled opportunities for new partnerships and allied services within sport, physical activity/education and health (Evans & Davies, 2015; Frisby, Kikulis & Thibault, 2004; Giulianotti, 2011; Robinson, Gleddie & Schaefer, 2016).

Whereas previously sport promotion may have been undertaken under the auspices of educational establishments, military or correctional bodies, sport organisations, charity and community entities, or physical educationalists, in recent decades corporate, private and philanthropic stakeholder interest and activity has grown (Frisby, Kikulis & Thibault, 2004; Press & Woodrow, 2005). Sport organisations (particularly those at the international and national level) have, for example, diversified from administrative practicalities to formalising links with educational providers and/or developed their own educational resource platforms. Recognised institutions such as the United Nations (UN), World Health Organisation, Red Cross, and Commonwealth Secretariat have also acknowledged sport as an important aspect of their respective missions (Kay & Dudfield, 2013; Meier, 2017; UNESCO, 2015; UNICEF, 2017). The charitable sector, too, has placed emphasis on sport as an educative tool for individual and social development (Goodwin et al., 2017; Harris & Houlihan, 2016; Lindsey & Grattan, 2012; Walker & Hayton, 2018; Wasser & Misener, 2016). Joining these groups are corporate entities who, either directly or indirectly, align sport education as a means of supporting economic, brand recognition and/or Corporate Social Responsibility (CSR) desires (Chelladurai, 2016; Levermore, 2010; Neesham & Garnham, 2012; O'Reilly & Brunet, 2013). Not only has interest grown, but so have stakeholder connections as entities look to address global concerns, share resources and expertise, develop strategies and policy, and ensure effective programme delivery 'on the ground'. Such is the current context that there are now an entanglement of global, regional and local entities demonstrating a unified commitment to universal humanitarian enterprise and delivering sport (and similarly physical education/activity, health and well-being) education *en masse*.

Underpinning this spectrum of activity, however, has been the (re)production of assumptions that synergise civic and moral values with sport practice. Namely, the sustainment of beliefs that sport has an inherent educational quality and an acknowledgment that the provision of sport (most often to young people) is a universally acceptable altruistic exercise that warrants our collective time, energy, investment and commitment. Such assessments are not, we respect, misplaced. Sport *does, can* and *may* do all this. Yet, equally, critique has also highlighted that the delivery of sport (as both service and product) and its integration (or incongruence) with the realities of peoples' lives and social spaces can be complicated and fraught with difficulty (Harris & Houlihan, 2016; Hayhurst, Kay & Chawansky, 2016; Lindsey, 2013; Mwaanga & Mwansa, 2013; Wilson & Hayhurst, 2009). Varying widely, tensions range from how individual and community needs are voiced to decisions over what sport provision entails, who might be involved and how organisational motives and imperatives are established and mobilised. Contestation also arises as power relations and hierarchies manifest; evaluation and monitoring mechanisms are decided upon; and ethical obligations, social responsibilities and concerns over 'sustainability', 'value' and 'meaning' are considered (Batty, 2016; Ferkins & Shilbury, 2015; Kombe & Herman, 2017; Mwaanga & Mwansa, 2013).

This book, *Sport, Education and Corporatisation: Spaces of Connection, Contestation and Creativity*, sits at this juncture. Advancing the previous concerns, we argue in this book that the issue has become one of not merely how and why sport is appropriated but rather understanding the powers and processes underpinning collaborations and decision-making, and the consequences, advantages and burdens that accrue thereafter. In terms of provision (and acknowledging coverage is still patchy, and many individuals and communities remain underserviced and under-resourced), we respect that having a plethora of patrons working to disseminate sport may be considered in positive terms. Beyond having innumerable sport education stakeholders, there are also a diverse range of policies, programmes, initiatives and resources being produced, and spaces being created to improve people's lives, experiences and communities. Work undertaken as part of the sport, education and corporate trinity, furthermore, now has a complexity that reconfirms and challenges ideological assumptions about what we know sport and education are and can be, and transcends sector and industry boundaries, state-private-charitable divisions, academic disciplines and geospatial terrain. There may be much to celebrate and hope in this work, yet such a proliferation and acceptance and privileging of some stakeholders and their activities, and the constantly changing sector landscape, also necessitate greater articulation and scrutiny. We commence, in this chapter, by establishing the general context, rationale, aims and intentions of our work. Following, we identify the book's theoretical, conceptual and methodological underpinnings. We then conclude by outlining some audience considerations and the subsequent chapter structure.

Our underlying thoughts

Sport, Education, and Corporatisation reflects our respective academic and disciplinary interests (particularly in the fields of Anthropology, Development Studies, Physical Education and the Sociologies and Histories of Sport). However, the book has also been developed in response to some of the issues raised by sector stakeholders that we have encountered in areas of the sport, development and education over the course of the last 13 years. In our efforts to understand individual and community experiences of sport across varied geopolitical and temporal terrain, we have witnessed an array of narratives and practices that demonstrate both the hopes and futilities of human agency, and the complex influences of structural and ideological forces. Our investigations have brought us in contact with students, teachers, organisations, corporations and communities for all of whom sport, physical education and physical activity have held some meaning or value (even if, albeit, that of disinterest, disengagement or ambivalence). These encounters have revealed the human and practical consequences of sports' inherent politics and politicising but also shed light on events, forces and structures, both seen and unseen, that affect and effect individual and collective day-to-day experiences.

What became evident through our formative research, and as we embarked upon this collaborative project, was a need for further interdisciplinary examination. Although we have investigated some of these issues within previous work (e.g. Collison & Marchesseault, 2016; Collison et al., 2016, 2017a, 2017b; Kohe, 2015; Kohe & Collison, 2019; Kohe & Newman, 2011), we identified a need to bring ideas from across our respective sectors of interest. In addition, we saw an opportunity to create a (re)generative ground for interdisciplinary and intersectional discussion. Informed by critical scholars from an array of academic fields, this book establishes an exploratory space that details some of the interesting, provocative, overt and subtle sector coalescences of thought, production and action occurring around us. We cannot, we respect, do justice to the enormity of the current sport industry's influence on peoples' lives, sport and education. Nor, for that matter, is it possible to articulate the full extent to which corporate and organisational intersections have embedded into sport education landscapes. However, what *Sport, Education, Corporatisation* does do is offer a new way to interrogate some of the prevailing sport, education and corporate connections, forces, structures, power relations and hegemonies currently evident in our societies.

We appreciate that readers now have an array of excellent texts available for examining sector issues. Nonetheless, while buoyed by this corpus of work, *Sport, Education, Corporatisation* responds to the need for a resource that focusses on, and privileges, connections between disciplines and domains of knowledge that are (at least in many of the institutions we have been a part of) often compartmentalised, certainly in terms of teaching and research areas. Accordingly, the book offers an original critical perspective by examining organisational initiatives within the context of an emergent Sport-Education-Corporate nexus. To this task, we draw on respective sociologies of sport and education, sport management, sport for development, geography, business ethics and commercialisation, and employ useful conceptual tools (including spatial theory, CSR ideals, critical pedagogy and care ethics) to provide a theoretically informed, empirically grounded framework to understand the development and proliferation of intersectional activities and related corporate partnerships in sport education. In so doing, *Sport, Education, Corporatisation* provides a valuable demonstration of ways in which educational-based imperatives and projects rationalise, normalise and justify alliances between sport organisations and corporate entities.

Intentions and aims

Reflecting our continued intersectionality interests, the intention of this book is to critique a recognisable interplay between sport organisational politics, educational development initiatives and corporate agendas. This triumvirate has become a powerful mechanism – and, essentially, an industry in its own right – of global(ised) sport humanitarianism, and this book endeavours to appreciate the nuances of its structure, reach, characteristics and effects. Scholarly attention has been afforded to the commercialisation of sport and education, respectively (Dyson et al., 2016; Harvey, Kirk & O'Donovan, 2014; Petrie, Penney & Fellows, 2014; Robinson, Gleddie & Schaefer, 2016), yet the Sport-Education-Corporate intersection (and specifically, corporate influence within the educational remits of sport organisations) has received limited scholarly attention. In part, the demand for such critique has been a response to distinct global, economic, social and educational forces (e.g. marketisation, sector privatisation, outsourcing, increased stakeholder presence within sport and education domains, state funding constraints and pedagogical reform). To varying degrees, such forces have fostered greater intersectionality between sport organisations, commercial stakeholders and formal and informal physical education/sport education developers and promoters (Dyson et al., 2016; Kohe, 2010; Lenskyj, 2012). For example, the International Olympic Committee (IOC); National Olympic Committees (NOCs); The Federation International de Football Association (FIFA); Premier League Football teams; UN and its affiliated sub-organisations; national sport federations; and companies like Nike, Adidas, Coca-Cola and McDonalds not only share various commercial and political alliances and goals but also have all demonstrated in some way (either through sport for development projects, creation of education resources or hosting public events) a unified commitment to education (Giulianotti, 2015; Kombe & Herman, 2017; Salcines, Babiak & Walters, 2013).

Frequently, relationships between corporate industry, sport and education are couched as part of understandable commercial and social responsibility imperatives. For example, corporations often subscribe to some form of an ethical or moral ideology, which usually manifests itself as an altruistic and humanitarian commitment toward 'communities', 'the public good', 'the environment/planet', 'children/ young people' or 'those most in need'. Sport (and relatedly physical activity and physical education), with its inherent value-laden and positive undertones, has been used often to demonstrate sport organisations' and corporate partners' shared commitment to a 'greater good'. Such imperatives are not inherently problematic. Yet the use of education (and commercialisation of projects within sport settings) also concomitantly serves to legitimise, normalise, promote and privilege sport organisations' commercial relationships and the presence of corporate involvement in educational spaces (Giroux, 2016; Kincheloe, 2002). As this book details, such is the extent of activity that the use of education/educational projects in sport has now become largely unquestioned as a means of meeting CSR ends and enabling corporate entities to politicise educational spaces for commercial ends.

Notwithstanding the attention given to some aspects of the Sport-Education-Corporate nexus in specific academic domains (e.g. neo-liberalism within Physical Education, commercial/stakeholder influence within sport organisational politics, corporatisation within Sport-for-Development and CSR within Sport Management), inter-disciplinary analysis of the nexus remains rare. Furthermore, current CSR critiques within sport scholarship have not focussed readily on the educational dimensions of commercial stakeholders' partnerships with sport organisations. *Sport, Education, and Corporatisation*, there-fore, fills this void. Accordingly, the aims of the book are twofold: (1) To provide evidential case studies that example the complex negotiations between stakeholder relationships within specific global, national and local spaces, and (2) to consider the potential social and ethical responsibility implications that emerge consequently to these negotiations. In crafting this book, we envisioned a book that could not only add to current understandings about sector stakeholders and their activities but also illuminate new and/or less-known connec-tions, relations and productions in and across the sectors. Our main objectives were:

• To provide an informed, interdisciplinary critique of the commer-cialisation of educational agendas within the sport industry.

- To interrogate some of the issues and challenges that emerge from the Sport-Education-Corporate nexus.
- To establish a valuable resource that can be used for interrogating ethical dimensions of contemporary sport organisations.
- To provide a discursive space to discuss future directions and alternative possibilities that challenge and/or provide a counterpoint to the prevailing Sport-Education-Corporate nexus trends.

This examination of the nexus offers a means to germinate important questions for the industry, and those who work within it, on undertaking research in its many aspects. Our own enquiry, for example, has been guided by several key questions. These have included: Understanding whose interests are privileged at the intersections; whose values are represented in the educational, commercial and political outcomes; how educational initiatives may be evaluated; upon what criteria (education, commercial or ethical) we might assess their various merits; and what the potential consequences might be for individuals, groups and communities that sports organisations and corporate stakeholders engage with. Reflecting scholarly influences that guide our thinking, we develop our examination around three key themes. Articulated further in Chapters 2 and 3, these themes are: (1) Sport organisational politics and the commercialisation of education within sport contexts, (2) the influence of contemporary global forces (e.g. globalisation, neo-liberalism and the ethos of social responsibility) on the corporatisation of (sport/physical) education domain and (3) CSR and ethics. These themes do not comprise or reflect all the idiosyncrasies of the nexus. Nor, for that matter, should they be understood in isolation to one another. Rather, we offer here a conceptual starting point to think about the ideological configurations that make the nexus possible, the knowledge productions and power relations that emerge therein and thereafter, and the potentialities for contestation and creative reimagining. Overall, we present *Sport, Education, and Corporatisation* as a way of acknowledging some of the characteristics and complexities that comprise the sector, identifying implicit and explicit intersectional connections, and appreciating how challenges to current stakeholder relations might be advanced.

Our approach

With the intention of exploring connections and relationships, our approach takes multiple forms. First, we acknowledge the need to consider advocacy spaces, stakeholder engagement, organisation behaviours and policy-maker influences at the global, regional and/or local levels. Such connections and relationships form, evolve and shift according to the space, time and nature of the process from inception to action. In harmony with this fluidity and our interdisciplinary approach, and in the manner encouraged by Gibbert and Ruigrok (2010), Toppinen and Korhonen-Kurki (2013), and van der Roest, Spaaij and van Bottenburg (2015), we adopt a multi-organisational case study approach that provides critical vignettes of sector activities and relations. Content is drawn from local and national educational curricula accessed from multiple international contexts (e.g. the United Kingdom, the United States, South Africa and South America). In addition, the book utilises sport organisation documents (e.g. those from the IOC, the NOCs, the international and national sport federation, the UN and charitable and development/aid-based entities), including publicly accessible material on policy initiatives, educational strategies and resources and sponsorship/CSR activities, available online or in organisational, higher education, secondary or government repositories.

The pursuit of examining both the philosophical/symbolic and the tangible connections and actions of the nexus necessitates an analytical design. Therefore, key actors, organisations and interventions and their connections are examined utilising a qualitative mixed-methods approach involving official curriculum document and policy analysis, commercial case studies, media critique, fieldwork and a priori engagement with industry stakeholders. While many of the primary documents and case studies already exist (particularly in terms of sport organisation and formal education initiatives), the novelty of this analysis is held in the commitment to tracing the process of establishing connections until the point of action. Recognition is also given to the often non-linear intertwining of spaces, time and processes. We have also interrogated various digital aspects and available online material, which supports and recognises the digital turn aspects that are now evidenced in both educational and sport development spaces (Sherwood, Nicholson & Marjoribanks, 2017). Ultimately, the case study approach is advantageous in allowing us to construct, interpret and reflect upon the intricate workings, management and outcomes of the nexus.

Organisation and structure

Congruent with our intentions, *Sport, Education, Corporatisation* has been organised as follows. Beyond this introduction, the book contains six chapters. The first two comprise substantive discussion devoted to underlying theoretical frameworks and contextual background for the research. We have divided the subsequent three chapters (Chapters 4–6) into global, regional and local spaces of thought, production and action. In the last chapter, we conclude by offering an assessment of the current state and characteristics of the nexus and potential avenues for future investigation.

In Chapter 2, we articulate the theoretical and conceptual frameworks used to examine the Sport-Education-Corporate nexus. Guided by scholars who have forewarned about the colonising powers of ideological and structural forces elsewhere (see, for instance, Evans & Davies, 2014, 2015; Giroux, 2015; Kivisto, 2016), our interest lays in articulating how hegemonic powers and ideas have contributed to organisational partnerships in the sport education domain. To these ends, we draw upon stakeholder theories and their utility for examining connections, responsibilities and expectations within the nexus. Here, stakeholder positionality, and a critical framing of CSR, is of value in assessing how intersection work is conceived and operationalised, and ways in which spaces (and by extension bodies) become occupied in corporate and ideological terms, and political authority and legitimacy manifest. Aspects of stakeholder theory and CSR, we acknowledge, are already used to evaluate areas of the sport sector. However, in this chapter we add nuance and structure to our conceptualisation of the Sport-Education-Corporate nexus by incorporating perspectives of spatial theorists (namely, Henri Lefebvre and Yi-Fu Tuan). Spatial critiques afford a mechanism to advance the practical and heuristic construction of the Sport-Education-Corporate nexus (specifically, the notions of 'thought', 'production' and 'action' that we employ in our analysis) (see also, Kohe & Collison, 2019). Moreover, spatial criticism provides encouragement to challenge the status quo of existing structural and ideological arrangements (in our case, the prevailing set of corporate interventions and alliances that permeate sport education landscapes). The spatial debates we draw upon also help us to understand how globalising agendas are produced, terrain is occupied and particular 'truths' about sport are constructed.

Chapter 3 establishes the broad context in which the sport-education-corporatisation nexus operates. The chapter recognises at the outset the significance of broader neo-liberal forces that have come to increasingly influence and characterise both the sport and education sectors (Davies & Bansel, 2007; Ford, 2016; Gulson, 2008). Noting current trends toward increased intersectional partnerships and activity (phrased often as 'outsourcing', 'privatisation', 'private-public-sector relations', 'venture philanthropy', 'external stakeholder engagement' ad nauseam), the chapter draws on a healthy body of scholarship that has long noted concerns over sport and Physical Education's corporate enmeshment (Dyson et al., 2016; Harvey, Kirk & O'Donovan, 2014; MacDonald, 2011, 2015; Petrie, Penney & Fellows, 2014; Robinson, Gleddie & Schaefer, 2016). We are, to note, less concerned here with the specific effects on active bodies than we are with identifying the structural and political components of the relationships of the Sport-Education-Corporate nexus and the consequences for social responsibility and ethical concern. There are inherent links to the making and remaking of bodies in these articulations, yet this issue lays beyond the intentions and focus of this book. Instead, the chapter establishes our position, which recognises the complex and contentious, yet at times necessary, corporate arrangements that sport and physical education have forged. Within this position, we consider that, although global contemporary conditions have challenged, changed and created opportunities, stakeholder connections warrant continued examination. Such investigations, we posit, may do well to employ the sentiments of critical pedagogues who advocate the sector need to privilege and make prominent commitments to social justice, empathetic ethics, agency and meaningful knowledge ownership.

The subsequent three chapters work from varying geopolitical levels of analysis. Of note, in adopting the geopolitical categories we respect that there is a significant degree of overlap, ambiguity and difficulty in defining their boundaries. To simplify, 'global', 'regional' and 'local' are, for us, amorphous referent points that, while generally understood as analytical and contextual units, are also organic, subjective and at times indistinguishable from one another. Our caveats here regarding fluidity across these geo-junctures echo the thoughts of our guiding spatial theorists Lefebvre and Tuan (discussed in Chapter 2). For our sake, these concerns play out in designating specific empirical examples to specific categories (e.g. in single initiatives and collaborations, organisations such as the IOC, FIFA, Nike and the Gates Foundation may operate and have impact across the global-to-local spectrum). Alternatively, organisations and stakeholder networks may strategically choose to implement initiatives specifically at the universal, regional/subregional or domestic levels. Nonetheless, organising our examples into global, regional and local is useful in highlighting what stakeholders may be operating where; the different sorts of connections that emerge at and across the various levels; how ideas translate into production and action; and, importantly, the similarities and differences in organisational relationships and practices across contexts.

These remarks withstanding, in Chapter 4, we focus on several large-scale initiatives of some Sport-Education-Corporate stakeholders. The chapter highlights ways in which recognisable corporate entities utilise sport and physical education to develop organisational scope, image and brand but more proactively seek to infiltrate sport education spaces to ply their trade. While certain companies have established reputations and condemnation for their practices (e.g. Nike, Coca-Cola and McDonalds), the chapter also examines how these global companies are joined by, and to, other public, charitable and private stakeholders. In many ways (e.g. with the formation of international policy and development imperatives), inter-sector alliances have produced discernible advances for sport education and individuals and communities therein. Nonetheless, such are the intricacies of some of nexus arrangements that it has become difficult to ascertain how relationships precisely work and where power, accountability, control and responsibility (and, at times, fault) may lay. Moreover, the ability that global companies have been able to yield in shifting international agendas and priorities raises questions about the receptiveness toward regional and/or local contextualisation and the meaningfulness of community representation, empowerment or ownership. We carry forward these ideas in the next two chapters.

In Chapter 5, we investigate how the Sport-Education-Corporate nexus maps onto regional/supra-regional contexts and how the globalising agendas of stakeholders (e.g. FIFA, the IOC and corporate philanthropic entities such as the Gates Foundation) are developed within distinct geographic spaces. While in many cases large-scale organisations have adopted international sport education approaches and initiatives that are in keeping with their global size and scope, there is value in these organisations refining their operations to the supra-regional, regional or local levels. In targeting regional contexts, organisations can (potentially) react to and mediate sociocultural, political and geographic idiosyncrasies to enhance programmes and stakeholder alliances. Through highly visible education projects, sport organisations and/or commercial entities can position themselves within narratives of 'positive' (as read in humanitarian terms) regional development. As some of the examples explore, in contributing to regional causes organisations may legitimise their place, and privileged stakeholder alliances, firmly within the geopolitical landscape. In so doing, power hierarchies become entrenched, structures of control normalised and mechanisms for representation and knowledge ownership shaped according to prevailing hegemonies.

In Chapter 6, issues of representativeness, ownership and knowledge construction are further rehearsed. Here, we examine how aspects of the Sport-Education-Corporate nexus are crafted within local spaces. Although, evidently, some corporate stakeholders have done well in engaging with local communities and taken into consideration nuances of the specific geopolitical domains in which they have chosen to operate, this is not always the case. Organisations may pay 'lip service' to matters of local engagement, consultation and partnership, yet issues of mutual benefit, meaning and relevance, agenda-setting, resource and knowledge-sharing, and control remain present. Prevailing scholarship, and sport and community development discourses generally, has frequently positioned such local corporate interventionism as inherently exploitative, inequitable and (therefore) unjust. Yet, in some instances, while dominant organisational stakeholders have had the capacity and resources to shape local priorities, local communities are not political dupes. Rather, there are intention, agency, opportunity and resourcefulness that exist at the ground level that can and do present an affront to total corporate domination. This chapter explores some of these possibilities and considers the possibilities for understanding stakeholder symbiosis *anew*.

Chapter 7 presents an evaluation of the Sport-Education-Corporate nexus and our initial work toward a typology of stakeholder types within the sector. Following an assessment of the book's examples, the chapter reconsiders the forces and values that have shaped education's corporate alliances and afforded commercial stakeholders a pronounced place in the politics of education design and implementation. We return here to the broader ideas of care, welfare, social justice, critical pedagogy and democratisation that drove our initial interest in developing this book. We stress our concern in being mindful of the construction and consequences of the Sport-Education-Corporate nexus. Furthermore, we reiterate our obligations within and beyond academia to continue to hold all stakeholders to account within the sector and to consider how sport education partnerships might sustain their ethical and empathetic intentions and values in the future.

Our potential audiences

In the first instance, *Sport, Education, Corporatisation* is a work directed toward scholarly audiences in respective Sport Management, Sport (for) Development, Sociology of Sport, Sport Policy and Politics, Physical Education and the wider Economics and Business Studies disciplines. The book is designed for students and researchers within these areas interrogating stakeholder relationships within the sport industry, sport organisational politics and practices, business ethics, commercialisation and corporatisation, CSR, educational and social development, ethics and social justice, sponsorship/endorsement within sport, global and international forces acting upon the sport setting, and/or neo-liberal consequences for sport/Physical Education. Beyond these obvious groups, and given its interdisciplinary nature, global-local focus and empirical evidence base, the book also holds value to those working within the wider sport and business sectors. The contents may resonate with those who work within corporate, educational, social and community development spaces. Such readers may identify with the issues of intersectionality, power and agency, structural and ideological forces, agenda-setting, contestation and creativity that are played out daily in their work. In addition, this book showcases the limits and opportunities related to addressing universal humanitarian concerns, fostering regional/supra-regional dialogue, confronting inequalities and engendering meaningful change and progress in sport spaces. Understandably, readers may take umbrage with some of our assessment and critique. Perhaps, for instance, with our fallibilities in not being able to do due justice to the contexts in which they reside; connections they witness; or realities that the nexus creates for their experiences, lives, work and communities. We return to these potential concerns in the book's conclusion when we encourage future research directions. Nonetheless, there is scope for *Sport, Education, Corporatisation* to be used to challenge current practices, encourage critical organisational reflection, improve relationship ethics and alter the sport sector for the better.

Conclusion

This work, we acknowledge at the outset, is not exhaustive, nor does it intend to map the entirety of the nexus dimensions and connections (such an exercise, we think, is futile). What we do provide is a way of thinking about how various aspects of the sport sector operate in concert to effect education and social development agendas. In emphasising the intersectionality of global-local stakeholder relationships, the book offers a unique exploration of collaborative work and agendas at play within the sector that have influenced sport, physical education, physical activity, health and youth/child discourses and practices. Within this broad church of connection there is, to note, much to endorse, respect and celebrate. We do not seek, for instance, to condemn unduly the prevailing ethos of neo-liberalism, capitalism or corporatisation that has wrought advantages and opportunities, created positive experience and changed lives. The examples offered herein attest to possibilities that exist within the nexus for stakeholder connectivity to be put to effective ends. Yet there are distinct and distressing concerns that warrant critical gaze, engagement and rebuke (e.g. spaces where stakeholder agendas and accountabilities are obscured, agency and freedoms are constrained or removed, or disadvantage may be exploited). Simply put, whether academic, student, practitioner or industry stakeholder, there is a *responsibility* and a *need* to interrogate, explain and challenge the sector and its capabilities. To this end, our hope is that the ideas presented within this book spark new considerations, critiques and contouring of the spaces in which we work, communities we inhabit and people with whom we interact. We trust you enjoy the read.

2 Theoretical and conceptual frameworks

Introduction

In this chapter we articulate the theoretical frameworks used to examine the formation of the Sport-Education-Corporate nexus. Our starting point is from a consideration of the sectors and entities interacting and occupying sport education spaces at the global, regional and local levels. Our interest here is in understanding not necessarily who stakeholders are at this point (this is covered substantively in Chapters 4–6) but rather how relationships emerge within the context of the corporatisation of sport education. In our previous and current work, we have witnessed the presence of specific colonising powers within the sector that have influenced agendas, occupied ideological and physical terrain, and utilised position and connections to legitimise authority. The construction of specific sets of stakeholder relationships has, we argue, had consequences for the production and dissemination of a set of 'universal' truths about sport (e.g. sport as 'peace building', 'sport-for-all', 'sport as empowering', 'sport for good', etc.). Here, an acknowledgement of stakeholders is of value in drawing out the importance of connections and synergies between global sport, education and corporate entities. In addition, by developing an appreciation of stakeholder connections it is possible to understand how political and ideological authority and power is exerted, collaborative work undertaken and issues of ownership and control negotiated and/or contested.

Within the wider context of sport education, it is possible to read stakeholder collaborations as purely humanitarian and altruistic. Such imperatives, nonetheless, often exist alongside or are inseparable from more strategic social responsibility agendas. Stakeholder relations, therefore, cannot easily be separated from an understanding of Corporate Social Responsibility (CSR). Respecting that the concept of CSR has received increased attention and mixed critiques within and beyond the sport sector, it remains part of the contemporary sport landscape. Through CSR it is possible to understand some of complexities of stakeholder relationships within the sector and, moreover, that there is a fine balance between the potential of CSR (e.g. to enhance organisational reputation and beget 'meaningful' community engagement) and development opportunities and leveraging (e.g. positive and sustainable social and economic improvement). We seek here not to assess CSR impact or effectiveness (as this is well accomplished by scholars elsewhere) but rather to conceptualise it as a nuanced characteristic of collaborative stakeholder ventures. An appreciation of CSR tensions and agendas leads us to consider also how the corporatisation of sport education might be (re)imagined and (re)crafted. Accordingly, we consider the composition of a new spatial commons. Drawing on the work of spatial theorists Henri Lefebvre and Yi-Fu Tuan, we present the construction of the Sport-Education-Corporate nexus, a holistic and heuristic notion of space crafted around the intertwined processes of thought, production and action.

Forging organisational alliances

The engagement of multiple sector partners within sport education spaces, and the orientation of corporate agendas to organisational alliances built around pedagogical sport practices, is easy to conceptualise within the standard frameworks of business. Stakeholder partnerships, and broader notions of connectivity, scholars note, may be contextualised as part of vibrant, dynamic, productive and progressive contemporary industry practices in which networks are formed; knowledge is exchanged; benefits are accrued; risks are shared; responsibilities are assigned; and individual and collective needs, goals and objectives are met (Nenonen & Storbacka, 2010; Zott, Amit & Massa, 2011). Although business imperatives vary, corporate effectiveness, efficiency and success work, in part, due to organisations capitalising on both their own resources and capacities, and leveraging the resource networks that they have at their disposal to accrue strategic and/or market gains (Corsaro et al., 2012; Hohenthal, Johanson & Johanson, 2014; Knoke, 2018). Resource sharing and partnership formation/network creation may not be an inherent part of all organisations' business strategies (particularly where contexts may necessitate organisational protectionism and aggressive corporate individualism), yet there is evidently benefit for organisations investing in relations that might serve individual or collective ambition. As rehearsed in Chapter 1, for example, the altruism and moral value entrenched in sport and education connections afford it a degree of recognised credibility as both a legitimate extension of business and a business in and of itself.

Invariably viewed as important, debates have emerged regarding stakeholder roles in the corporate structure, identity and operations of organisations (Jensen, 2010; Knoke, 2018). Beyond interrogation of what constitutes the stakeholder (Bryson, 2004; Miles, 2012, 2017; Werther & Chandler, 2010), critique has also taken interest in the characteristics, functionality and approaches to stakeholders within contemporary business models and organisational operations (Carroll & Buchholtz, 2014; Tantalo & Priem, 2016). Of value here is the need to recognise the multifarious places that forging stakeholder relations has in driving sector activities toward shared corporate ends (and/or a 'greater good'). The interest in stakeholders does not dismiss other dimension of business activity (e.g. economics/finance, administration, management, logistics and ethics) but rather seeks to situate stakeholders either at the centre, or toward the centre, of discussions about corporate frameworks (Davies, 2016). As such, and moving beyond articulating who stakeholders are, our approach examines the nature of stakeholder relations across the intertwined sport, corporate and education domain. In addition, we examine how organisations formulate and sustain connections, whose interests relations serve and how those interests are serviced, what the moral and ethical obligations of stakeholders are within common projects, and in what ways power, conflict are hierarchies are manifest and contested.

Scholarly critique transcends these initial concerns, yet the underpinning theoretical guidance is valuable in acknowledging idiosyncrasies evidenced in stakeholder networks. Moreover, there is encouragement to interrogate implicit and explicit ways relations contour corporate cultures and connectivity. It is this intellectual thread we carry through in identifying and evaluating stakeholders' configurations within the Sport-Education-Corporate nexus. As rehearsed in other business spheres, it is the fundamental value of partners and partnerships to operationalising shared organisational agendas in sport that draws us to consider stakeholder debates and conceptual analysis of corporate partnerships (Bridoux & Stoelhorst, 2014; Donaldson & Preston, 1995; Freeman et al., 2010; Greenwood & Van Buren, 2010; Miles, 2017; Russo & Perrini, 2010). In articulating a Sport-Education-Corporate nexus, it is evident that spaces of connectivity comprise varied stakeholders working simultaneously toward individual and collaborative aims (Greenwood & Van Buren, 2010; Miles, 2017). Stakeholder relationships, for example, may be contingent upon the nature and characteristics of the collaboration space (e.g. international, national or local focus of sport projects), assumptions about organisational remits and the parameters of delivery (essentially, who does what, when, where and how), ethical considerations regarding social and cultural obligations, and wider ethical questions about trust, duties of care and long(er) term sustainability (Oruc & Sarikaya, 2011).

A stakeholder cognisant approach offers a means to appreciate the intricacies and contradictions within organisational interactions, the politicisation of sport spaces to serve assorted agendas and the inherent associations between corporate practice and ethical community engagement. Collectively, theoretical stakeholder explorations facilitate critique of how aspects of the sector currently operate and draw attention to possibilities of industry change (e.g. encouraging ethical stakeholder behaviours that might better resonate with local/community recipients) (Friedman, Parent & Mason, 2004). Within the sport sector, an explicit focus on stakeholders makes sense. Consider, for instance, the complexity of sport network structures (Coalter, 2013; Friedman, Parent & Mason, 2004; Houlihan, 2016; Preuss, 2015); the spatial and temporal contexts across which sport organisations work (Sotiriadou, 2009; Van den Hurk & Verhoest, 2015); the varied commercial desires of corporate entities in the sector (Ferkins & Shilbury, 2015; Frisby, Kikulis & Thibault, 2004); the communities sport serves (Evans & Davies, 2015; Green & Smith, 2016; Harris & Houlihan, 2016; Martin et al., 2016); and the territoriality of relations that traverse public, private, charitable, (quasi-)non-governmental and political spheres (Anagnostopoulos et al., 2017; Batty, 2016; Ferkins & Shilbury, 2015). In investigating these issues, research on stakeholder relations within sport has primarily come from three disciplinary perspectives: Namely, sport management, sport policy and the sport for development/sport development sectors.

With respect to sport management, attention here has been to stakeholders as a fundamental constituent of corporate sport culture (Cody & Jackson, 2016; Ferkins & Shilbury, 2015; Peachey et al., 2015; Vance, Raciti & Lawley, 2016). Under the context of capitalism, scholars note that both the professional and public sport sectors are driven by, and drive, mechanisms of profit maximisation, labour exploitation and alienation in the pursuit of efficiency, constant consumerism, wealth accumulation orientated toward upper tiers of ownership, and trends in operations and practices that blur lines between 'good' governance, revenue production, business ethics and corporate and/or social responsibility (Andrews, 2016; Collins, 2013; Harris & Houlihan, 2016). While debate and focal points vary, a commonality of criticism has emerged with respect to the breadth and depth of corporatisation that is imbedded within modern sport across the globe. Moreover, there has also been a unity of concern with respect to the extent to which corporate notions now shape more directly what sport *is*; *how* it 'looks' and 'works'; *where* agendas are directed; and *whose* purposes, profits and pockets it ultimately serves.

The existence of corporate sport (Andrews & Silk, 2018), per se, is not necessarily detrimental. Indeed, some scholars have pointed to the multifarious advantages corporate trends have had improving production, patronage, promotion, public engagement and experience, and sector sustainability (Andrews & Silk, 2018; Hayhurst, Kay & Chawansky, 2016; Mills, 2010). Rather the issue here, and point explored in forthcoming chapters, are the degrees to which corporatisation ideals and forces have become entrenched and normalised in diverse areas of the sport industry. With the progression of corporate maxims, furthermore, there are notable implications and consequences for stakeholder relationships that matter for the general conduct of effective business and the exercise of power over, and connection with, the consumer audience businesses purport to serve. Stakeholder critique and theory, thus, is of use in illuminating the ways in which corporate thought and action is shaped and enabled, and the ways in which sport organisation works in concert or incongruence with partners along the fine line of managing successful business operations and evidencing ethical behaviour.

Within sport policy, concerns with stakeholders have been evidenced in both the nature of the policymaking landscapes at local, state and global levels, and the multilayered, intra-related and interwoven ways in which the iterative cycle of policy formation occurs (De Bosscher et al., 2015; Goodwin & Grix, 2011; Houlihan, 2014; Weed et al., 2015). While this corpus of work has been measured in its applications of stakeholder theory, the critiques have adopted congruent positions regarding the precarity and/or synergies of sector relationships. One remit has been providing workable conceptual frameworks that better account for policy dynamics and stakeholder roles therein. In the United Kingdom, and not unlike elsewhere, for example, the domestic sport policy scene has been articulated as comprising an array of actors (e.g. the respective State departments for Culture, Media and Sport, Education and Health; educational providers; non-governmental agencies such as the Youth Sport Trust and Sport and Recreation Alliance; charitable organisations; and other private- and public-sector entities) (Green, 2009; Houlihan & Lindsey, 2012; Piggin, 2015). Although these stakeholders do not all assume equal or similarly valued roles within policy processes, the formation cycle necessitates levels of various engagement as the process moves through conception, implementation and evaluation phases.

Stakeholder consideration within policy practice, scholars note, does not occur naturally. Nor, for that matter, is stakeholder involvement rarely benign or without consequences. In numerous countries considerable efforts have been made in some corners of sport/ physical education policy development to better utilise stakeholder involvement (Stenling & Fahlén, 2016; Van den Hurk & Verhoest, 2015). Part of this activity has entailed state departments responsible for sport, physical activity and/or physical education delivery, for example, forging strategic alliances (often precipitated by budget cuts and strapped resource allocation). Various connections, thus, have been established with Higher Education providers, curriculum developers, charitable sport and non-sport organisations, and the private sport and leisure sector who may act as policy activators/implementers, non-governmental entities as consultants and advisors. Concomitantly, corporate sector links serve to provide commercial support, dissemination opportunities, branding and marketing, and public engagement throughout the policy process (Collison et al., 2016; Harris & Houlihan, 2016; Sotiriadou, 2009). By its very nature, sport policy is stakeholder cogniscent and reliant. Notwithstanding the necessity of stakeholders within this sphere, what matters here is how policy works with, for and to stakeholder means and ends. An appreciation and articulation of stakeholder theory draws attention to initial emergent, and eventual, roles and responsibilities that constituent parts undertake within policy work; the extent to which varied organisational (read also: business and corporate) agendas can be mapped on to policy construction; and (dis)harmonies that may be evidenced when policy ideals and practices differ and thus disrupt stakeholder relations.

For our purposes, the interrogation of stakeholders in the sport policy domain has been fundamental. Namely, in underscoring the characteristics and components of policy cycles, identifying key policy phases that draw stakeholders together, interrogating ideological discourses that inform and disrupt policy processes (e.g. health and well-being ideals or participatory versus competitive sport agendas), continuities and contiguities of stakeholder approaches across sport spaces, and ways in which power and hegemony manifest in policy connections. With respect to understanding the Sport-Education-Corporate nexus, such concerns help form our realisation that, irrespective of the existence and strengths of partnership and processes, there are few guarantees in sport spaces. As such, there remains a responsibility to prevail in examinations that interrogate rhetoric and claims of stakeholder unity (especially when that unity is contoured by, and purports to exist in tandem with, corporate interests).

The concerns vis-à-vis stakeholders raised within the policy sector are also found within Sport-for-Development and Sport Development domain. The development sector (whether domestic, regional or global) is a political and politicised space in which colonisation, occupation, accommodation, resistance and negotiation are frequently contested and contestable. Respecting subdomain distinctions (Coalter, 2010; Hartmann & Kwauk, 2011; Hayhurst, 2011), scholars here have long noted that the developmental territory both within sport and beyond is predicated upon the establishment of multilateral, multi-spatial, and multi-organisational partnerships and networks to survive (Burnett, 2015; Coalter, 2010, 2013; Hayhurst, Kay & Chawansky, 2016; Smillie et al., 2013). Stakeholders (particularly large entities such as the International Olympic Committee (IOC), The Federation International de Football Association (FIFA), and supranational constituents such as the UN and United Nations Educational, Scientific and Cultural Organization (UNESCO)), for example, are players who yield unfathomable power and influence in shaping discourse, attention, resources and outcomes, and the pace and place of these choices. Although capable on their own, these organisations fortify their work and presence by establishing strategic partnerships based on shared ideals and actions (e.g. the UN Development Goals, Red Cross operations, World Health Organisations objectives or IOCor FIFA aims). These stakeholder connections sit resolutely as part of the contemporary sport framework. Nonetheless, there is the need to assess underlying political and power issues that frame and enable these prevailing sets of relations. Scholarly criticism usefully warns of the need to be wary of being seduced by the efficiency and external congruence of stakeholders' connections within the sport development sector (Levermore, 2010; Levermore & Beacom, 2009). Moreover, while countenance to hegemonic sport development stakeholder structures may be possible, the participation of smaller, less-resourced, peripherally positioned entities is contingent on continued advocacy (Coalter, 2010; Lindsey & Grattan, 2012). Reflective of these concerns, a stakeholder focus provides a means to critique notions of stakeholder synergy and capacities for organisations to redress inequities in partnership relations.

The aforementioned scholarship serves to legitimise our conceptualisation of the Sport-Education-Corporate nexus and the utility of considering stakeholder dynamics in and through its formation. There are, admittedly, theoretical limitations. Scholars have, variously, noted the marginal attention afforded to organisational agency and business ethics, the overemphasis placed on the effectiveness and productivities of relations, and the difficulty in accounting for relations within a holistic understanding of the corporate industry (Wagner Mainardes, Alves & Raposo, 2011; Miles, 2017). Mindful of these as we proceed, nonetheless, we see merit in incorporating an appreciation of stakeholder theory within our interrogation of sport spaces. Following those who have already drawn attention to the tensions between stakeholders' effects on business, we also see value in exploring ways stakeholders connect within the Sport-Education-Corporate nexus. Part of our interest also lays in understanding how business operations intertwine with ethical considerations (a point we consider in Chapter 3 when addressing how an ethics of care might aid in transforming spaces of sport into sites of moral action).

CSR considerations

In examining sport, education and corporate connections, we appreciate the place ethics (specifically, discourses of moral responsibility) may/may not have within stakeholder relations. Concern for ethics within the broader corporate sector has, for example, conventionally been articulated within the concept of CSR. The term itself has created much debate, with early definitions including and rejecting social, economic, legal and ethical expectations of corporations and how such perspectives both align and disconnect to the broader role of business in society. During the 1980s and 1990s, further conceptualisation gave enhanced complexity to the field, intersecting alternative themes of stakeholder theory, business ethics theory and corporate citizenship (Carroll & Bucholtz, 2014; Davies, 2016; Friedman & Miles, 2002). Definitional issues withstanding, the point is that business organisations have increasingly been expected to demonstrate a greater contribution to society via social, educational and environmental activities (Salcines, Babiak & Walters, 2013). In part, this trend has also been a consequence of high-profile failures in corporate governance, accountability and transparency and reformed measures of corporate performance (Clarke, 2004). CSR now carries diverse meanings and perspectives in both business and sport sectors, and it is with these complexities in mind that we consider how CSR brings both global sports businesses and non-sport organisations into the sport education thought spaces, interactions and productions.

The growing prominence of CSR within and through sport has been argued to reflect the unique features of sport itself (Westerbeek & Smith, 2005). Sport tends to have, for example, a strong philanthropic appeal and is frequently seen as an effective vehicle for deploying CSR programmes or for disseminating educational and development objectives (Giulianotti, 2015). Moreover, the positioning of sport as a universal phenomenon and recognised human right constructs overlaps of thought between the respective social and educational responsibilities of sport organisations and corporate entities. As Smith and Westerbeek (2007) argue, sport exposes social responsibilities which implicitly form connection and mutual opportunities to leverage their identities, development priorities and agendas. It is through the construction of partnerships, Levermore (2010) further suggests, that CSR and sport demonstrate the strength of their connection.

Giulianotti (2015) categorised four positions of CSR in sport as: CSR within sport, strategic development policies, developmental interventionist policies and social justice policies. This framework highlights the diverse spectrum of CSR activities that may be pursued by corporations and the wider role of sport for various social and educational pursuits. Importantly, organising CSR in this way exposes the numerous stakeholders, non-governmental and state actors that form connections and networks when undertaking social and educational agendas. With this framework in mind we should note the complex and diverse audience and participants embedded in CSR-sport-education work. For example, Nike's sponsored 'Skillz' HIV awareness programmes in South Africa have involved partnerships with elite athletes, private and national health sectors, NGOs, international charity organisations and non-state and state actors. This programme also represents strong connections to global and local strategic developmental, and interventionist health and educational policies. This form of philanthropy and/or commercial soft power agendas can be mistaken as an overly simplistic coalescence to reach mutual goals. However closer examination exposes the consequences diverse stakeholders have in these spaces.

CSR should be, Giulianotti (2015) suggests, subject to critical reflexivity so that new knowledge can be generated to explore alternative models and depoliticise the tensions of neo-liberalism evident in sport partnership work. CSR and the utility of sport for education have been exposed to significant programme evaluation; in part this may be due to the somewhat awkward coming together of contrasting philosophical and ethical standpoints. There is also the concern of sport education programmes being poorly linked to core business objectives, leading to disconnect that threatens the credibility of projects and impact. As scholars forewarn, philanthropic partnerships based on ideals of social good and education sit uncomfortably from a purest standpoint. This is most prominent when CSR supports educational initiatives aligned with sport mega events. For example, corporations who sponsor the Qatar World Cup have had to respond to worker's rights abuses, environmental concerns and human rights issues. Therefore, we might suggest that in the act of funding sport for the purpose of social good and education, there is potential for reputational risk which is at times heightened by commercial branding, marketing and their physical presence on the ground. The partnerships formed through CSR allow an element of protection from on the ground evaluations, but the need to showcase 'doing good' exposes commercial investment in complex environments that may by association carry controversy.

Creating a spatial sport commons

In addition to the aforementioned guidance, the conceptual development of the Sport-Education-Corporate nexus is also aided by a philosophical appreciation for the complexities of space. Social scientists have been drawn to notions of space to interrogate physical and cultural practices, individuals, communities and wider territories (Jansson & Koch, 2017). Debates withstanding, discussions have recognised the relative, fluid, deep and interdimensional nature of space and its ability to be conceived in both a holistic and a practical sense (Jones et al., 2014; Müller, 2015; Studdert & Walkerdine, 2016). Sport scholars, too, have valued space as a concept for exploring a range of physical, political, historical and social issues and phenomena (Bale & Vertinsky, 2004; Van Ingen, 2003). Sociologists of sport, for example, have placed emphasis on the global, local and glocal characterisation of specific spaces (Giulianotti, 2011; Malcolm, 2012). Additional work has critiqued spaces of sport mega events and assumed harmonies or disjuncture(s) with the localities in which they are entrenched (Gaffney, 2008). Further scholarship has explored physical aspects of distinct sporting, physical activity and leisure environments (Pretty et al., 2005). Collectively, such accounts evidence degrees to which sport is interwoven into geopolitical landscapes, the significance of sport practices to specific spatial groups and the relevance of space as a construct to 'work with' in social research. Informed by this research, our use of space begins not initially from a point of physical space but from acknowledging space as a heuristic device and a holistic way of understanding an intersectional commons. Our interest is in conceptualising a philosophical space in which sport, education and corporate practices meet.

Building on previous sport scholars examining space (Van Ingen, 2003), we are guided by Henri Lefebvre's (1991a, 1991b) encouragement and calls for a critical appreciation for space as a metaphysical construct. Lefebvre's work comprises a valuable basis upon which a deeper understanding of space and its meanings may be advanced (Lefebvre, 1991a, 1991b, 1996, 2003; Lefebvre & Réguiler, 1986/2004). Taking umbrage with uses of the term orientated around structural, institutional, economic and geopolitical bases (and, thus, understandable in materialistic terms), Lefebvre (1991b) reconfigures space (or *l'space*) as transitional (effectively, as a site, or set of sites, in which people, goods, ideas and communities are in perpetual motion). For Lefebvre space transcended the urban (and thus the physical) dimension. *L'space,* Lefebvre argued, was an active entity – a site of constitutive meanings and actions that are simultaneously geographic, social, temporal, physical and interdimensional, consolidating, crystallising and crumbling continuously. Lefebvre was not necessarily suggesting such a consideration of space belied tangible interpretations. Instead, Lefebvre proffered a warning about the difficulties, and futility, of endeavouring to 'capture' space and deduce its meaning. What mattered, rather, was the necessity of highlighting the cultural basis and complexities of space and demonstrating appreciation for notions of change that are inherently and innately part of spatial transformation and (re)configuration.

Lefebvre, we respect, was not necessarily suggesting that holistic understandings of space were divorced from the practicalities of the physical dimensions. Rather the obverse: That spatial renderings are affixed to social, political and geographic referent points. Lefebvre's expression of *L'space* is of value in understanding how the Sport-Education-Corporate nexus forms in an intellectual, virtual and transcendental sense (and operates independent of temporal or spatial specificity) but also for explaining and using the nexus for articulating the realities of everyday lives and communities in situ (Sheilds, 1999). By developing the conceptualisation of space to incorporate metaphysical expression, Lefebvre makes it possible to also move us beyond considering space in terms of production, and move, rather, toward discussing space as 'a tool of thought and of action' (Lefebvre, 1991, in Gleseking et al., 2014, p. 289). We explore ideas of action later. We underscore here, however, that adopting a Lefebvrian approach to space allows us to consider not only what a Sport-Education-Corporate nexus might 'look' like but how its philosophical dimensions might become real, practical and consequential.

Yet, with regard to the rhetoric and reality of a spatial commons within the context of sport, it warrants being mindful of Coalter's

(2013) warnings to be 'suspicious of any convenient convergence of self-serving interests with the greater good' (p. 4). The common belief systems and objectives of those tasked with selling the idea of sport, raising standards or opportunities for education and producing or funding such ideas as a source of social responsibility, Coalter notes, have increasingly been criticised as 'evangelist' in tone. As such, articulations and evidence of spatial synergies (either in thought, production or action) necessitate caveats, if not a modicum of scepticism. Respecting Coalter's position, we nonetheless share Sheilds's (1999) appreciation for Lefebvre in that such theorisation highlights the fluidities of space and spatial connections. Moreover, these theoretical directions also enable consideration of the cultural, deep, interdimensional and virtual meanings of space. Here, the spatial ground we are articulating is a one formed upon shared humanitarian ideals about community, belonging, citizenship and pedagogy. Specifically, for the Sport-Education-Corporate nexus, these ideas and principles are based on working collectively 'for the greater good' or 'public good', 'doing good', 'contributing to civil society', 'enhancing communities' and serving 'children/young people' or 'those most in need'.

The Lefebvrian dimension of the Sport-Education-Corporate nexus is furthered by the seminal work of Yi-Fu Tuan (1977). As a genesis to Lefebvre's work, and centred on ideas of openness and freedom, Tuan's examinations add nuance to understanding the transcendental, philosophical and abstract nature of space. For Tuan, space is most importantly a metaphysical construct deeply connected to thought, emotion, feeling and embodiment. Taken in unison Lefebvre and Tuan encourage an approach to space that begins in the ether, takes shape through cultural practice, social interaction and physical connection, and is made visible through modes of production. Such principles, and the notion that space is indelibly tied to a commonality of thought and action, inform our work with the Sport-Education-Corporate nexus. From Tuan and Lefebvre's inspiration, we offer nexus as a collective commons, that is, at first, a metaphysical space in which sport, education and corporate *thought* collide, create possibilities of *production* and generate opportunities for creativity and *action*.

The symbolic process of sharing common ideals and engaging in collective spaces of *thought* and advocacy is the initial phase of constructing the nexus. For stakeholders to effectively connect and have meaningful presence within spaces, connections must go beyond ideals and into the realm of interaction and production. *Production*, in contrast, serves to manoeuvre commonalities, objectives and resources to establish spatial power, leadership and hierarchies among stakeholders.

Our interest lays in articulating stakeholder positions and connections that, while orientated around commonality of altruistic *thought*, are symbolically charged and power-laden. While inherent hegemonies exist within the nexus, resistance, reappropriation and unsettling of power relations and hierarchies may be possible in some spaces. Appropriately, it is useful to draw on Lefebvre's notion of the 'the third space'. For Lefebvre, the third space encapsulated how peoples' lived experiences were a culmination of the processes of thought and production (Sheilds, 1999). Characterised by *action*, the intention of the third space was transcendental and transformational, that is, to create possibilities for community enterprise and, potentially, revolutionary reactions and new knowledge forms (Sheilds, 1999). In the case of sport education initiatives and corporatised sport programmes, *action* entails taking produced meanings and resources and translating them in ways that resonate within specific locales. A consideration of *action*, therefore, aids understanding how spatial transformation and reconfiguration might occur and knowledge and meanings altered to fit specific, and familiar, discourses and ideals. Explored via *thought*, *production* and *action,* essentially the Sport-Education-Corporate nexus can be conceived as a dynamic entity and system of ideological and practical connection, intersectional agency, power and struggle, and localised meaning making.

Conclusion

Although useful, we acknowledge here that the theoretical pathway we have articulated is not exhaustive, nor does it fully allow for all practical aspects of the nexus to be examined. We also appreciate the triumvirate we propose sits alongside a substantial conceptual family of similar cross-sector connections (e.g. sport-corporate-media, media-sport, military-industrial, sport-military-industrial, higher education-sport-corporate complexes) (Batts & Andrew, 2011; Giroux, 2015; Giulianotti & Armstrong, 2011; Whitson, 1998). All of which (whether nexus or complex) have spurned needed debate about multi-sector (m)alignment, the politicisation of space, political reappropriation of industries for just and unjust causes, and the entrenchment of cross/intra-sector collaboration into contemporary public life. Nexus articulations effectively demonstrate how sector unities or conflicts are created, operationalised and sustained within and across particular settings. In doing so, conceptually the notion of a nexus is a reminder of the explicit and implicit connectivity that constitutes our collective and individual social realities. Furthermore, a nexus provides a means to evidence the ends to which these networks are enacted in the pursuit of distinct agendas and the maintenance of specific power relations and political hierarchies. Our conceptualisation offer is a platform to explore Sport-Education-Corporate connectivity and provides some clarity, focus and perspective on a terrain that is difficult to comprehensively capture in space and time. Connections between stakeholders, for example, consistently shift; ideals and values change and morph; places of organisational investment move in accordance with geopolitical, economic and humanitarian needs; corporate entities grow and shrink; educational providers realign policy; charitable agencies come and go; and community demographics alter. In drawing together stakeholder, CSR and spatial theories, we respect that these notions of change and continuity are actively part of the phenomena we interrogate. Thus, the nexus (such as we conceptualise there being one) is thought of not as a static juncture but rather as a practical and ideological confluence that bends as part of the modernisation and progress of sport business. We offer up the Sport-Education-Corporate nexus as a heuristic device that might help an interdisciplinary and holistic critique and move us to new sites of action and opportunity (in the manner critical pedagogues discussed in the next chapter envision) that work within and transcend current humanitarian challenges.

In the chapters that follow we provide an initial explanation of how the Sport-Education-Corporate nexus might be envisioned. As discussed at the outset, although substantive work has been undertaken by colleagues on specific and individual components, and some of the dual connectivities, (e.g. corporate-sport, sport-education and the corporatisation of education), our work provides a contribution that attempts to bring these respective elements together. We begin by exploring how the creation and maintenance of the Sport-Education-Corporate nexus has been predicated on the capitalisation on, and corporatisation of, people's sporting and active lives, and turned their respective communities into sites of corporate consumption (Harvey, Kirk & O'Donovan, 2014; Holt, 2016).

3 Capitalising on play

The corporatisation of sport/ physical education spaces

Introduction

This chapter provides an appreciation of the Sport-Education-Corporate nexus context and its consequences. Focussing on stakeholder partnerships, and connectivity of thought, production and action, we consider there to be value in understanding how corporate and educational agendas coalesce around sport spaces in the pursuit of profit and system efficiencies, market place domination, sustainability, brand and image management, and political power. The point here is not with a rebuke of capitalism or with its continued existence in shaping sport. As we explore through the chapter, and book generally, the corporatisation of sport is not necessarily always problematic. Within the Sport-Education-Corporate nexus, capitalist neo-liberal influences are largely undeniable, in many cases unavoidable, and have been frequently venerated. Sport, education and corporate stakeholder connections have, for instance, produced advantageous opportunities and outcomes for young people and been effective in providing global platforms to advocate community concerns. However, the commodification of sport, physical education/activity cultures and spaces has also constrained individual or collective liberties, freedoms and choices; created (and perpetuated) conditions that have exacerbated existing inequalities, inequities and power relations; and contributed to hegemonic discourses that cannot be (or are difficult to be) challenged and changed (Kivisto, 2016; Slater, 2015; Torres, 2008). As extant criticism regarding neo-liberalism and capitalist logic in sport/ physical education has warned (Evans, 2014; Evans & Davies, 2014, 2015; Penney, Petrie & Fellows, 2015; Williams & MacDonald, 2015; Wright & MacDonald, 2010), current conditions may prevail, yet the corporatisation and commodification of sport must be held to greater account and its potentially deleterious effects countered.

While our interest is on a critique of physical and sport education spaces, discontent with the forces shaping education around the world has already been notable and extensive (Amsler, 2011; Cote, Day & de Peuter, 2007; de Lissovoy, 2008; Freire, 1992, 1994/2014, 2000, 2001, 2016; Giroux, 2003, 2004, 2005, 2007, 2009; Kincheloe, 2008a, 2008b). This work has radically shifted educational paradigms and advocated strongly for interventions that disrupt current practices and provide new ways of thought. In broad terms, critique has drawn attention to, variously: The challenges to educational democratisation; the consequences of neo-liberalism and neo-liberal agendas within the sector; the constraining colonisations of minds and bodies (particularly those of young people); the threat of commercialism/corporate interventionism; and the necessity of reorientating pedagogical projects back to spaces that are empathetic, equitable and empowering (Ball, 2012; Blum & Ullman, 2012; Giroux, 2011; Lipman, 2015; Picciano & Spring, 2012). We take these sentiments forward in this chapter and examine how within the prevailing context 'rights' to physical/sport education have been re-acquisitioned and repositioned as corporate prize, fuel and fodder.

The corporatisation of education

The universality of education and the recognition of educational rights are well-established and have resulted in a raft of international and domestic laws and statutes (e.g. UN Convention of the Rights of the Child (UNCRC) (UNGA, 2007; UNICEF, 2015, 2017). In many cases (as some of the examples in this book highlight), the recognition of education has been instrumental in ensuring improvement to access, equality of opportunity, individual and community development, and advancing the quality of educational experiences and attainment (most recently evidenced in the *Education 2030 Incheon Declaration and Framework for Action*, UNESCO, 2015). Yet, as extensive as efforts have been to ensure the democratisation of education, the processes and conditions in which these rights are played out are significantly contested. Accordingly, while it may be legitimate to assert individuals' claims to *an* education, this claim to ownership, experience and opportunity does not necessarily extend to securing participation in educational spaces or preclude educational spaces from corporate colonisation. Notwithstanding the formal structures and establishments operating at state levels, in practical and ideological ways educational territories from the local to global remain fair game, that is, sites that (if not sufficiently protected) may be utilised, positioned, appropriated, occupied and claimed by and for any number of entities (and ideas) (Ball, 2012; de Lissovoy, 2008; Giroux, 2017). The presence of varied stakeholders, and that stakeholders may exert varying degrees of ownership over educational terrain, is, scholars assert, a concern (Blum & Ullman, 2012; Lipman, 2015). The issue stems, in the first instance, from the configuration of the education sector as part of a space in which free-market imperatives can prevail and pedagogical content can be commodified. As part of this, 'education' becomes objectified and, therefore, acquirable for the stakeholder/ stakeholders who can leverage the best resources (e.g. political, financial, ideological capital) toward its acquisition. Although contributing to improvements in educational provision, experience and access, increased stakeholder presence has still functioned to treat education ownership in competitive market terms. Such a position may be easily understood and accepted. The trends witnessed in relation to the Sport-Education-Corporate nexus, for example, are symptomatic of the wider sector and the general degree of indifference it has shown toward increased occupational infiltration.

The educational shifts toward corporatisation and the acceptance of the sector to corporate partnerships and/or multi-stakeholder alliance, and participations in educational design, have not emerged suddenly (de Lissovoy, 2008; Giroux, 2009, 2016; Kivisto, 2016; Lipman, 2015). Rather, alterations have been precipitated by enduring and contemporary political, economic and social conditions. Essentially, "as neoliberal strategies are shifting production from a nation-state function to a global one", Blum and Ullman (2012, p. 372) note, "the form of the human being is changed and challenged by new uses of education". Comparable to other sectors, in education, "new practices of exclusion and enclosure are contracting political space into monopolised zones of exclusive activity" (Amsler, 2011, p. 48–49). Over recent decades, this state of education has been lamented (Amsler, 2011; Kivisto, 2016; Olmedo, 2013; Sandlin, Schultz & Burdick, 2009; Torres, 2008). Scholars have drawn specific attention to the malaise the sector has faced over the course of the 20th and 21st centuries, and the necessity of reconfiguring education at its core as an emancipatory project (Burbules & Berk, 1999; Giroux, 2011; Kincheloe, 2008b; Saltman, 2012). We will return to these ideas later. For now, we consider a few of the underlying intellectual sentiments apropos education space, ideological and practical colonisation, and the positioning of (young) peoples' pedagogical experiences as for sale without consent (Amsler, 2015; Lipman, 2015; Saltman, 2012; Slater, 2015).

Although explainable as part of the progression of modernity, the educational sector has been placed in a position where its ethos, intentions, core values and missions remain increasingly difficult to protect. As educationalists warn, it is not just the sector's complicity in its own colonisation (as evidenced and made possible by the erosion, in some countries, of school funding, resourcing and support; concomitant difficulties for charitable providers; and a valuing of shifts toward market imperatives [e.g. employability, key industrial skill development, business training]) (Amsler, 2011; Blum & Ullman, 2012; Kivisto, 2016). Rather, what matters is that when education is configured in this way or in these terms, its purposes fundamentally change. Individuals may not, to note, stop learning, engaging and experiencing (and that all this might not be positive and/or beneficial). As evidenced shortly, out of the corporatisation of education have come new pedagogical initiatives that have educational value in inspiring young people and invoking the social conscience many critical educationalists advocate. Nonetheless, what is at stake and being compromised is what is learnt, to what ends engagement is put, what experiences ultimately accrue and how experiences are appropriated in corporate terms (or more simply, branded and framed vis-à-vis Corporate Social Responsibility (CSR), social philanthropy or community investment). This may seem strong criticism, but, as seen in the coming chapters, these concerns are being witnessed more frequently in various corners of the sector.

Capitalising on play and a recall to critical pedagogy

While degrees of recognition around the globe may vary considerably, sport and physical education have been acknowledged within formal and informal educational settings as meaningful (Evans & Davies, 2014, 2015; MacDonald, 2011). Such recognition may in large be due to ingrained and long-held social and cultural assumptions regarding the myriad benefits that may potentially accrue to individuals, communities and wider society in and through developing peoples' physical capacities. The transformative potentialities of sport and physical education notwithstanding, the sector has not been immune to the effects of corporatisation. For some time, scholars have taken umbrage with the reorientation of the discipline of Physical Education and sport writ large for ulterior causes (Evans & Davies, 2015; Penney, Petrie & Fellows, 2015; Williams & MacDonald, 2015). Their critique has extended beyond just corporate imperatives and encroachment to consider a wide range of consequences and concerns that emerge from neo-liberal largesse and excess. Discontent with the status quo has been levelled not just at Physical Education but also more broadly at related realms of sport, sport education and physical activity.

The ability and the capacity for corporations to engage in sport and education projects have been aided by the shifts that have opened spaces (e.g. schools, sports clubs, charitable development entities and training providers) and created conditions for the flourishing of multi-organisational partnerships and knowledge exchange, and global-local initiative production (Coburn & McCafferty, 2016; Lenskyj, 2012; MacDonald, Hay & Williams, 2008). In countries such as the United States, the United Kingdom, Australia, New Zealand and Norway, neo-liberal reform has provided opportunities for curriculum development, content diversification, public-private partnerships and increased 'choice' and 'freedom' (Dowling, 2011; Evans & Davies, 2015; Penney, Petrie & Fellows, 2015; Powell, 2015, 2018). Not unlike in other sectors, this territorial reshaping had entailed: Closer alignment between physical literacy and social skills development within curricula to key market and industry skill sets, increased synergies with business/industry/corporate partners and closer working with a wider array of stakeholders beyond the educational realm, financial support and branding of curricula and learning resources, growing outsourcing of content development and provision to external 'specialists', and the reconfiguration of young people's sport and physical experiences as marketable activities (Culpan & Wigmore, 2010; Gard, 2015; Powell, 2015; Whipp et al., 2011).

Against a backdrop, in some cases, of state-disinvestment into communities, people and their education, such changes to the discipline may be easily welcomed. This may be particularly the case where tangible benefits are seen with regard to peoples' experiences, increases in physical activity and sport participation, enhanced learning and developmental opportunities, curriculum enrichment, economic and social investments into local communities, and/or relief being provided for under-resourced and over-stretched schools and practitioners. While from the disciplinary standpoint, scholars argue that free-market orientations present fundamental challenges to subject content, knowledge and pedagogy forms, teaching practice and stakeholder engagements, there is something more at stake that transcends formal learning contexts and constituents (Evans & Davies, 2015; MacDonald, 2011, 2015; Wright & MacDonald, 2010). What appears to matter is that contextual trends have turned the pursuit of educational enlightenment into a market enterprise. To this end, and at its most basic, Physical education and sport (and the values and ideals that it comprises) become commodifiable and 'fair game' for those who can leverage resources to its acquisition.

Cogniscent of these concerns, it is useful here to draw upon and take inspiration from the long-established stream of critical pedagogical debate that has been instrumental in advancing education's wider functions and transformative potential with respect to social justice, empowerment and emancipation (e.g. Ball, 2012; Blum & Ullman, 2012; Darder, Baltodano & Torres, 2003; Ford, 2016; Freire, [1994]2014, 2016; Giroux, 2005, 2016; Kincheloe, 2002, 2008a, 2008b; Marcuse, 1968, 1975; Nichols, 2016). Debates here have largely condemned the ways in which neo-liberalism has contributed to the diminishment of the establishment and disconnected the provision of education (that is, who teaches and who is taught) and development of pedagogy (what is taught, how it is taught and why) from clear and compassionate ethics (guided by the needs of those who purpose(s) the education purports to serve). Critical pedagogies, Amsler (2011, p. 53) offers, "enable people to become conscious of their repressed desire for freedom and empower them to act in informed ways to improve the conditions of their existence". Such an education, at its heart, should afford opportunities for people to recognise and enact upon injustice but effect sensitivities, sensibilities and capabilities to enact change (Burbules & Berk, 1999). This is, in essence, the core of the critical pedagogical project. However, as Giroux (2016), Gulson (2008), Lewis (2006) and others have continued to note, it is not enough just for critical pedagogy to radically challenge curricula, engage communities, address moral concerns, liberate minds and disrupt orthodoxies; it must instil in people (in our cases all stakeholders within the Sport-Education-Corporate nexus) the value that taking such action is possible *and* meaningful.

We respect, of course, that critical pedagogy is not a new concept. We also knowledge that others have advocated more extensively, strongly and long(ingly) for its causes. This work, however, has provided a useful political catalyst for thinking about educational reconfiguration within the Sport-Education-Corporate nexus. We do not deny, also, the importance of corporate crafted pedagogical projects that may make human experiences and lives better. Nonetheless, we take forward the essence of the debates regarding the need to challenge hegemonic forces in education that, implicitly or otherwise, are exploitative and/or constrain or limit freedoms and empowerment at the local, community and individual levels. These considerations of educational composition, ownership and ethics are central to understanding the nexus and broader issues of corporate stakeholder occupations in sport spaces.

Stakeholder colonisations and the education shadow state

The corporatisation of the sector has created space for entrepreneurial entities to lay claims and craft the sector to their own causes. One context in which this has been evidenced is within the United States. In recent decades, critics note, the intervention of corporate agendas and motives within educational governance, advocacy, provision and curricula in the United States has notably increased (Hackworth, 2007; Kivisto, 2016; Lipman, 2015; Picciano & Spring, 2012). The spread of corporate educational interventions has not, however, been universal across the sector or the nation. Rather, interventions have emerged at spatial and demographic junctures that have had the most amiable conditions for marketisation and commercialisation. As Lipman (2015) identifies, frequently these conditions have been a weakened (State) education sector, inequities in the balance of State educational resources versus those of external capital investors, sustained federal and civic underinvestment that has made education sites and communities susceptible to alternate governance, and the rapid growth of corporate desires for new markets and audiences. Although the corporatisation of education has adopted many guises, Lipman's (2015) specific interest is with regard to the operations of one set of corporate agents, that of venture philanthropists: Essentially those individuals/sets of individuals (and their associated altruistic entities) who seek out educational spaces as a means to expand their charitable service (framed also as corporate/social responsibility).

Venture philanthropy, for Lipman, exemplifies the landscape of neo-liberal educational colonisation. Namely, that their presence may be expected under the logic of capitalism, yet the manifestation of their power creates a concern for the pursuit of democratic educational enterprise (Davies & Bansel, 2007; Giroux, 2016; Hackworth, 2007). Drawing on case studies of Detroit, Philadelphia and Chicago, Lipman (2015) illustrates how venture philanthropists (e.g. the exorbitantly wealthy Gates, Walton, Broad and Ford Foundations; also discussed further in Chapter 5)[1] strategically situate themselves at the forefront of State education investment, renewal and governance. This positioning has been made possible not only by the internal shifts within education governance but also by substantial civic disinvestment, economic malaise and wealth inequities that have weakened schools and communities' capacities to resist the attractive proposition of philanthropic investment (Kivisto, 2016; Lipman, 2015; Olmedo, 2013; Peck & Tickell, 2002). Reflecting the occupation of the educational commons evidenced by others (Ball, 2012; Giroux, 2004, 2011;

Olmedo, 2013; Picciano & Spring, 2012), venture philanthropists have commandeered educational spaces such to the extent that discernible influences can be seen across several areas. For example, in school governance, policy creation, project funding structures, underlying business imperatives, the focus of pedagogical and social initiative development, and the reappropriation and communication of their educational investments within their commercial branding (Lipman, 2015). Activity has also comprised of corporate sector support and interjection in curriculum development, situating 'appropriately minded' business intellectuals within educational governance, positioning corporate educational products/services in amiable market terms and pushing the development of charter school networks (Hackworth, 2007; Lipman, 2015; Scott, 2009).

The proliferation of venture philanthropists, and the corporatisation of education more generally, has historical trajectories. Echoing peers' remarks about the long march of corporate colonialism (Ball, 2012; de Lissovoy, 2008; Giroux, 2003, 2011; Olmedo, 2013; Scott, 2009), Lipman notes how current power relations within education have been rooted in hegemonies of White settler colonialism, capitalist expansion, industrialisation processes, social control and pervasive power inequalities. Notwithstanding the complexities of contextual forces, the arguments advanced here are that corporate foundations have been complicit in agendas to pacify, control and dictate the populous via 'education' domination. Such is the pervasiveness of venture philanthropists, Lipman (2015, p. 242) points out, that they now effectively constitute and operate as a 'shadow state'; a collective and nuanced force of organisations operating in surface and subterranean ways at confluence of public and private spaces to effect (or, in this case, control) sector alteration and intent (Mitchell, 2001).

At the foundational level, Lipman's (2015) interrogations demonstrate that there is something fundamentally disconcerting when unelected corporate entities are afforded legitimacy in State governance and policy formation. As wider debates articulate, it would be easy to accept this all as au fait accompli: Part of the new, unavoidable, epoch of entrenched corporatisation and sector monopolisation. This may be an accurate assessment. Yet there exists a concern not only for the contemporary state of education, and the governance of peoples' minds and bodies, but also for inherent values that may lay at the core of the education and pedagogical projects in the future (Amsler, 2011; Kivisto, 2016; Torres, 2008; Williams & MacDonald, 2015). The corporatisation of education should be decried, scholars contend, and people should be protected from ideological domination, excessive

State control, exploitation, unfounded censorship, inequity, injustice, suffering and harm (Cote, Day & de Peuter, 2007; Davies & Bansel, 2007; Giroux, 2011; Olmedo, 2013). Ultimately, the assumption within this critique is that peoples' education (the young in particular) still constitutes a sacred space that should be fortified, defended and incorruptible (Ball, 2012; Blum & Ullman, 2012; Burbules & Berk, 1999; Freire, 2007, 2016; Giroux, 2003). Addressing these calls for the redirection of education shortly, we turn now to consider how corporatisation has manifested within physical education/sport space and had consequences for class and social power.

Physical pedagogy, class and social power

While a full conceptual evaluation of power lays beyond the scope of this chapter, it warrants noting there that power in the context of social capital, mobility and class is politically charged. Inevitable top-down bottom-up approaches and competing agendas, for example, are constant sources of power negotiation and contestation (as highlighted across Chapters 4–6). Therefore, class and social power need to be considered from both an institutional and a structural perspective and intervention standpoint. It should also be acknowledged that power and class are connected, and it is often through the realisation of collective commons and the coming together of separate entities to enact change that power and class are both exposed and exercised. As detailed in the forthcoming chapters, power within the nexus maybe presented in diverse forms and is most obviously acted upon at the top policy making and custodian levels of the corporate, sport and educational sectors. Under the labels of influencers, advocates, decision makers, leaders and policy-makers, it is 'power' that places individuals and groups into such positions and maintains organisational hierarchies and relations.

With the coming together in the nexus of three distinctly powerful groups, establishing global leadership or forming hierarchies between funding sources, key sport stakeholders and state and/or non-state actors is not only a political pursuit but a social class enterprise.

Recognising the deeper symbolic qualities of physical practices, Bourdieu (1978) reminds that sport (and related educational) practices are inherently class based and it is through observed connections that sport can be understood in relation to class, embodied capital and the practice of power. Class and power coalesce in the nexus through the positioning and exhibition of economic strength. In relation to top-down bottom-up nexus relations, for example, issues of class manifest in the privileging of, often Global North, voices that negotiate and dictate agendas on the behalf of the less-privileged, less-advantaged, absent target populations (Banda & Gultresa, 2015; Darnell, 2010; Smith & Westerbeek, 2007). In this way, the corporatisation of sport/physical education comprises a moral dimension that brings into question issues of care and ethics which philosophically contrast to the founding ideals of education for all (Hayhurst, 2011; Hayhurst, Wilson & Frisby, 2011). Research has, moreover, long suggested latent forms of power and class discourses are enacted within Physical education, including hidden social concepts, patterns and characteristics, which reinforce hegemonic ideology that serve the interests of dominant groups (Evans & Davies, 2015; Fernandez-Balboa, 1993; Robinson, Gleddie & Schaefer, 2016). Once Physical education agendas surpass traditional curriculum and delivery spaces, the injection of corporate influences bring further concern and critical issues into the fold.

Sport/physical education are spaces in which power is negotiated through physical dominance, establishing of roles and hierarchies, access, aesthetics and embodied performances of class, gender and skill (Maguire, 2011; Renold, 1997). Often at the detriment of the social justice and empowerment frameworks which focus sport education programmes, for example, Anderson (2009) argues that power and dominance issues are institutionally codified within sport and are reproduced by stakeholders who often neglect cultural norms. In addition to this, target populations are automatically positioned as socially marginal and disenfranchised and this has consequences for the dynamics of educational interventions at the local level (Nicholls, Giles & Sethna, 2011). Physical education and sport for education programmes, therefore, expose local class dynamics between those that 'do' and those that 'can't'. Regional or local practitioners and implementers, for instance, may adopt facilitatory roles between the top and the bottom organisation levels, and be afforded recognition for enacting social 'good'. Yet, as this position may be reliant on external funding sources and assumed 'the power of sport' to achieve goals, such a position may be considered fragile or unstable. In our forthcoming analysis, we acknowledge class and power relationships and dynamics that are institutionally embedded across the global to local levels and that shift according to the context and thought, production and action phases.

Critical pedagogies by way of an ethics of care

In the tenor of critical pedagogues, we argue that the Sport-Education-Corporate nexus emerges at a juncture in which spatial borders have become ever more porous, stakeholder engagements endorsed and rewarded, and peoples' minds and bodies conceived as legitimate occupational terrain. Yet we respect that such a configuration is not immutable to change, challenge or corruption. If this is the case, then there is potential for redirection. In response to the commodification of education, and corporate prevalence, for instance, possibilities for resistance, activism, emancipation and empowerment exist that essentially might liberate people from staid educational models and hegemonies. Examples here include alternative school models that afford young people greater agency and ground-up interventions that capitalise on local knowledge and experience; adapting pedagogies to better reflect peoples' lives; and destroying bureaucratic measures that are reductionist, oppressive and exploitative (Amsler, 2011; Nichols, 2016; Slater, 2015). We rehearse these ideas again in later chapters when we consider how the Sport-Education-Corporate may manifest and be enacted in certain spaces. Before this, it is useful here to consider how ethics (in this case, an ethics of care) might underpin our calls for redirection.

Discussions of activities and partnerships within the sport education sector have not generally attended to care ethics as an essential characterisation of collaboration. Consideration can, however, be found in comparable sectors (e.g. health and welfare services) (Held, 2006; Pettersen, 2011; Tronto, 1993). Here, work has emphasised the necessity of developing care as central to business/industry practice. Notions of care ethics are defined by and orientated, variously, around values of enhancing welfare and well-being, respect for individual dignity and rights, and protection from harm and suffering. In terms of the sport industry, corporatisation of education and stakeholder synergies, ethical care theorists remind us that at the core of business are human relations and that all human relations comprise of moral and ethical dimensions. Furthermore, although each stakeholder may possess varied perspectives on their own and other's moral obligations, there exist points of shared collective beliefs that merit respect and protection (think here, e.g. of the differences between the values and objectives of sport educationalists, corporate programme sponsors, philanthropists, state agencies and sport organisations). In sport such beliefs typically manifest as commitment to human flourishing, social and cultural development, the promotion of collective and individual health and well-being, and protection from harm and suffering (IOC, 2017; McEwan & Goodman, 2010; Oruc & Sarikaya, 2011; Pettersen, 2011).

As seen in sport/physical education, among sport organisations, and with sport development projects, an ethics of care may already be at work (though it may not always be visible). Stakeholders in some spaces, such as the IOC, FIFA and UNESCO, and corporate entities, for example, already espouse commitments to humanitarian development and social responsibility as part of their underlying philosophy. Nonetheless, translating philosophy into practice (and in the case of the Sport-Education-Corporate holding *all* stakeholders to their ethical and moral obligations) is difficult, and there are no guarantees an ethics of care will be afforded the same value as part of the business of 'doing' sport business. Nonetheless there is scope, we believe, for care ethics to be central to stakeholder connections and to be evidenced better and more explicitly in the development of physical/sport education initiatives. Our intention here is to encourage readers to not only consider the value of an empathetic and emancipatory education but also appreciate the role care ethics may play within Sport-Education-Corporate critique.

There is, also, another means in which care ethics can be articulated. In addition to being framed as an educational space, the nexus is a part of the larger sport sector. The operations and identities of its constituent parts (e.g. sport organisations, corporate entities, educational providers), and the connections between stakeholders, can and are understood in business terms. Moreover, to be effective, efficient and sustainable, business partnerships are contingent upon partners demonstrating a basic level of care toward each other (or at least provide an indication to care). This may be expressed as developing mutual trust, respect, cooperation, transparency, accountability or more generally as 'good' governance. Regardless of stakeholders' individual agendas and intentions, notions of care may be considered vital. Drawing connections between the moral and business imperatives of the sport industry in this way raises useful questions about, variously: What care 'looks' like in the nexus; whether, in the pursuit of neo-liberal sport industry agendas, there is a legitimate rationale to care; which stakeholders demonstrate care and why; what the care constitutes and what its limits are; how care is politicised by stakeholders; and what, if any, are the consequences of care for stakeholders (especially young people) when ethical obligations fail (Koggel, 1998; Koggel & Orme, 2010; McEwan & Goodman, 2010; Sevenhuijsen, 1998).

By introducing the notion of care, we present an attempt to bridge the ethical dimensions and debates associated with the sport industries business operations, models and approaches with the social ethics that are deeply entrenched within critical pedagogy discourse (and by extension that which is found within sport/physical education advocacy). Guided by critical pedagogues, we believe there are opportunities for care ethics to be deployed in critiques of the corporatisation of sport/physical education (particularly in drawing attention the effects capitalist processes have on peoples' lives, experiences and welfare and the responsibilities and obligations stakeholders have to one another). As will be explored in this book, care ethics is at the heart of a genuine critical pedagogical spirit and may be of value in when (re)orientating actions with spaces. To this end, we take additional inspiration from those scholars (e.g. Boler, 2004; Boler & Zembylas, 2003; Cote, Day & de Peuter, 2007; Lewis, 2006) who call us to acknowledge existential realities yet remain steadfast in our commitments to pedagogical hope and the pursuit of utopian horizons.

Continued considerations

In totality, these critiques amalgamate a substantive set of concerns regarding the current state and possible futures of education shaped by largely unchecked, undemocratic and unaccountable free-market enterprise. Such critiques hold utility in the effort to better understand the state of play for sport/physical education projects at the global, regional and local levels and the issues that may arise in partnership junctures. Within the context of the Sport-Education-Corporate nexus, this matters for a variety of reasons. In the most general sense, and rehearsing Lipman (2015), Coburn and McCafferty (2016) and Kivisto (2016), while it might be possible to see the inevitability of neo-liberalism, the domination of education by its agendas (as witnessed through acts of corporatisation) remains demonstrably undemocratic. That is, that the processes of corporatisation, by its nature, does not fundamentally embrace nor accept the principles of equitable representation and participation (e.g. within governance, agenda setting or initiative implementation). To clarify, and drawing upon the discussion outlined in Chapter 2, there are inequities that inherently exist within partnership formation and an inevitable power bias that accrues to the more well-resourced party/parties. Under the tenets of neo-liberalism, market place domination and sector control (such as that sought out in the various philanthropic foundation activities undertaken in the United States) feeds on the creation of an inequitable competitive sector in which investments can be made, terrain occupied and gains made. As has been argued, such is the case that in some locations schools, informal education providers, communities and individuals/groups play increasingly restricted roles in this process. To varying degrees, opportunities for educational decision-making have become released from institutional, conventional and state moorings and become more easily placed in corporate hands.

Wholescale corporate control may be some way off (we hope), yet control over the provision of sport/physical education remains susceptible and its ability to withstand corporate occupation precarious. As explored later, there are benefits to furthering public-private partnerships in the sector. However, to recall Lipman (2015) and Mitchell's (2001) notions of the 'shadow state', the continued creation of educational frameworks shaped by (and for) private industry is worrisome as it normalises corporatisation as *the* modus operandi (potentially also, as often in the case of IOC-UN/UNESCO-corporate partnerships, as a model par excellence). The degrees to which this may or may not be acceptable (and this, we respect may depend entirely on spatial context and recipients' ethical orientations) warrant further debate. Nonetheless, the notable wealth and resource that is currently being mobilised by a variety of corporations (and/or their philanthropic foundation branches) in the name of education presents a considerable form of power that is difficult for governments and communities to ignore or counter effectively. Moreover, as laudable or necessary as these private-public stakeholder arrangements may be, they ultimately mask corporatisation as benign altruistic philanthropy and social responsibility when there are evidently commercial and business imperatives being advanced. These points, to note, are also comparable to those that have long been echoed in the sport development and peace corner of the sector (Coalter, 2010; Giulianotti, 2011, 2015; Kombe & Herman, 2017).

Either as a tool, process, product or practice, sport holds value to corporate stakeholders wishing to stake a claim upon educational commons. The ability of corporate stakeholders to harness sport to business ends and means, and to exert influence, power and control over sport/physical education spaces, may be (at least in part) due to the inherent sociocultural and ideological qualities and characteristics sport is assumed to imbue. For example, think here about the frequent assertions about sport developing character, sport as fundamental to human endeavour and experience, sport as a humanitarian practice, sport as integral to harmonious individual and civic development and enlightenment, and sport as a valid human right (FIFA, 2017, 2018; IOC, 2017; UNESCO, 2015). These hegemonic discourses may abound, yet they have also been effectively capitalised upon by stakeholders who have leveraged the affective power of sport to garner support and acquiescence to their causes. Invariably, corporate entities (in allegiance at times with education providers and sport organisations who, too, accept sports' ideological doctrine) have deployed sport as an inclusive ruse to engender complicity, compliance and control (ubiquitous positive assertions such as 'sport for all', 'sport for peace', 'sport has the power to do 'X'', 'inspire a generation' through sport, etc., attest to this idea). What happens here is that there is a naturalised alignment between corporate entities to sports' popularism, positivism and secularism in a way that repositions their takeover of education as unobtrusive and inoffensive.

Overall, what the tightened consolidation of corporate involvement has achieved is in the creation of a context in which certain stakeholders are able to dictate the terms and conditions of sport educational initiatives and processes, and, moreover, wed initiatives to outcome driven accountability measures that may not be achievable, sustainable or congruent with communities' and individuals' needs or desires. Following these arguments through to practical realities, what is also of concern is that corporatisation also places participants as mechanisms of a grander political and economic narrative toward ends which they may have no interest in, awareness of or capacity to resist. As seen in the subsequent chapters, from global to local spaces, corporate entities have utilised considerable economic, practical and political resource to ensure that initiatives are commercialised in attractive ways that make ideological and practical 'buy-in' a near certainty, and stakeholder intervention as the default status quo. Without necessarily the knowledge or intention to do so, corporatisation also positions individuals' sporting participations, educational experiences and community cultures as not merely just occupiable spaces but occupiable without consent. Recalling Lipman's (2015) earlier remarks about stakeholders' exploitation of de-invested communities, questions of consent are problematic. In some cases, the contextual forces may constrain consent considerations. In some sport education spaces, for example, the attractiveness of corporate interventions may place individuals and communities in difficult positions, whereby they may simply be 'out-resourced' and have little choice but to yield to corporate colonisation (particularly if they wish to maintain imperatives to improve lives, welfare and social development goals).

Scholars' sustained scepticism has highlighted the continued necessity of interrogating the ability of the education sector to withstand and/or 'work with' neo-liberal forces, institutions and practitioners' capacities to arrest the progression (or diminish the disadvantageous effects) of corporate practices and the value of rescuing peoples' hearts, minds and bodies through critical pedagogical reconfigurations. We recognise that while the context of neo-liberalism and corporatisation of the sector merits attention, it is evident that there is no universality of solutions that can be sought here. Furthermore, we appreciate that in the complexity of education provision these concerns we have outlined may not be shared among stakeholders. Rather, what we seek is to consolidate and fortify critique of the sport education industry and provide a catalyst for positive change to thought, production and action. We take these ideas forward in the subsequent chapters when considering who operates in sport education spaces and why, and what is at stake in terms of the values underpinning peoples' educational experiences and pedagogical development.

Conclusion

This chapter has provided a discussion on some key elements enmeshed within the Sport-Education-Corporate nexus. Building on the politicisation of space and the complexities of stakeholder relations explored in Chapter 2, we drew attention to debates regarding the corporatisation of education, the commodification of peoples' sport/physical education and the countervailing academic encouragement to challenge hegemonic practice through ethical, just and compassionate pedagogies. We established some initial connections here to demonstrate how, conceptually, the nuances of the Sport-Education-Corporate nexus might be broached. Our articulation underscores the value of considering the intersectionality of the nexus and the merits of adopting an interdisciplinary framework of enquiry. In addition, the chapter explored how stakeholder congruence and spatial colonisation within the nexus are premised on a set of specific ideological assumptions vis-à-vis humanitarian ideals (e.g. notions of a common good, sport as a valid right, etc.). As such, therein lies an ethics of care to its causes. Duties of care, however, are easily eroded (or made peripheral) in the quest for stakeholders to achieve commercial or ideological imperatives. If this is the case, as part of a radical decolonisation of space at the point of action, a (re)turn to critical pedagogies may be needed. As we rehearse toward the end of this book, these pedagogies are unlikely to begin necessarily from organisations and corporate entities (as part of a universalising or global doctrine) but rather may best be shaped by individuals' and communities' desires.

Note

1 These foundations represent the most significant corporate charitable entities operating within the United States. The foundation's remits, scope and reach, however, extend beyond the United States into a variety of international spheres. Such are their individual and collective contributions, that they yield considerable political power over the shape of global educational and frame sector priorities and hold sway over the stakeholder relations

and representation and legitimacy of activities and spaces of investments. All four foundations currently make substantive investments into a range of sport, physical education and activity initiatives as part of the varied global policy and advocacy agendas. Moreover, while foundations frequently espouse apolitical stances, their organisational support traverses community, state, regional, supra-regional and international levels and projects in ways comparable to other large-scale development entities such as the EU, UN, UNESCO, World Health Organisation and Red Cross (https://www.gatesfoundation.org/; https://broadfoundation.org/; https://www.fordfoundation.org/; https://www.waltonfamilyfoundation.org/).

4 The Sport-Education-Corporate nexus

Global cases

Introduction

This chapter highlights the varied ways that sport, education and corporate connectivity may manifest at the global level; which we have interpreted by adopting a focus on large-scale, multinational/multi-sector entities whose reach traverses and transcends national boundaries. It should be noted, however, that given the organic and dynamic nature and development of partnerships and initiatives it is difficult to do justice to the breadth and depth of organisational players and their activities. The intention here is to provide insights into current relations and practices evidenced in the sector, and bring to light ways in which thought, production and action coalesce. In doing so, it may be possible to acknowledge how corporate connections with the state and/or the third sector (e.g. community and charitable entity) have contributed to operational hegemonies in the colonisation of sport and physical education spaces. While cross-sector alliances and interdependencies have yielded results in provision and development terms, they have also been effective in normalising sector approaches. This normalisation also extends to related assumptions about the constraints of the state to deliver sustainable ventures, 'vulnerabilities' of the community and charitable contributors, and the inabilities of the sector to operate in lieu of corporate interventionism. Such ideas frame this chapter and the subsequent chapters that examine regional and local operations. Drawing on examples from Nike, McDonald's and Coca-Cola, we consider first some points of global thought coalescence.

Global thought

The following examples encompass several well-known, large-scale, culturally entrenched global enterprises. As explored in Chapter 3, corporate participation and political interjection into sport education are not necessarily novel. Nonetheless, the current examples evidence not only the growing interest that corporate entities have shown in adopting positive associations to sport and physical education enterprise but also the extent to which organisational commitments have become ideologically and practically intertwined with larger cross-sector partnerships and global health, well-being and welfare campaigns. Apart from work interrogating public health governance (Harman, 2016; McCoy & McGoey, 2011; Rushton & Williams, 2011; Yancey et al., 2009) and work scrutinising localised philanthropic sport initiatives (Neesham & Garnham, 2012; Piggin, 2015), there remains the need to articulate these global stakeholder relations.

Nike

Nike's prominence as a global brand and its continued marketing activities, celebrity contracts, sport-mega event associations, technological innovation and widespread popular appeal have afforded it recognition which has aided its power as a corporate contributor to social and community development (Burgelman, 2017; Kornum et al., 2017; Mahdi et al., 2015; Merk, 2015; Rowe, Karg & Sherry, 2018). Similar to other global entities, sustaining market prominence has entailed Nike demonstrating commitment to corporate values (particularly in terms of accepted standards of 'good' governance) but also civic altruism that illustrates to customers and investors that the company has meaningful moral bearings. Nike is, of course, not alone in its efforts. As rehearsed in Chapter 2, while organisations have engaged with Corporate Social Responsibility (CSR) for varied means and ends, such actions and investments are part of companies' wider strategies to demonstrate synergies (or mitigate incongruences or disharmonies) between 'doing' business and the overt and covert practices of 'how' that business is done (Bryson, 2004; Smillie et al., 2013; Van den Hurk & Verhoest, 2015). In Nike's case, persistent criticism has been leveraged at its questionable business and ethical practices vis-à-vis labour exploitation (Giulianotti, 2015; Knight, 2007; Rowe, Karg & Sherry, 2018). Although Nike has alleviated some of these concerns (e.g. by creating the *Nike Community Impact and Ambassadors* programme, https://communityimpact.nike.com/nca, an initiative to incentivise employees to give back to communities), responses to developing sustained ethical practices have been laboured (Bartley & Kincaid, 2016). The point here is not to focus on Nike's integrity as a business and employer per se but rather to consider what Nike *is* doing, and what capacity large companies like Nike have *to do*, within sport education spaces.

One of Nike's prominent initiatives has been the *Designed to move* project (http://www.designedtomove.org/; Piggin, 2015). Now well established, the conceptual basis for the project began in 2010 when Nike led a multi-sector and international collaboration of sport, physical education and physical activity industry stakeholders to confront the 'growing epidemic of physical inactivity'. The consortia's overall intentions were to consolidate empirical evidence, formulate effective public policy and develop a unified strategic action plan that might catalyse long-term, sustainable, demographic change. To aid its credibility and legitimacy as a physical (in)activity provocateur, Nike gained academic endorsement from the American College of Sport Medicine (ACSM) and the International Council of Sport Science and Physical Education (ICSSPE). Nike's financial input was matched with economic support from The Clinton Foundation, Inter-American Development Bank, Special Olympics and International Amateur Athletics Federation (IAAF). The initial 70+ contributing organisations were later joined by an additional 73 organisations (from international to local level, commercial, State, charity and education providers). The initial output was the production of the official *Designed to Move: A Physical Activity Action Agenda* Report (2013; http://www.designedtomove. org/resources/designed-to-move-report). In addition to providing data for policy development and implementation, the report comprised actions, strategies, suggestions and encouragements to catalyse social and cultural change at the local, national, regional and international levels (Piggin, 2015). The report illustrates how the notion of a collective commons (or commonality of thought) may be achieved irrespective of the sector boundaries, parties' individual intentions or local geo-temporal/social/political or economic inequities. While inherent differences may exist within consortia partners and in initiative development, monitoring and evaluation, there is evident unity of intellect, purpose and intent within the report that reads as persuasive discourse (and contributes to already established discourse). Such coherence presents itself as a strong, substantive and compelling unity of thought that may be easily 'bought into' by other stakeholders.

As one example of translation in the sport education sphere, the report has informed activities and partnerships within the United States-based *'Let's Move Active Schools'* programme (https://www. activeschoolsus.org/). Involving multilateral and multi-sector partnerships and investments, the programme delivers resources, technical support and professional development to all United States schools and provides young people physical activity opportunities and enhanced learning experiences and environments that might sustain long-term physical activity engagement. In addition, Nike also invests directly into the *Let's Move* initiative (https://about.nike.com/pages/sport-and-physical-activity--2). The report has also been used to leverage the participation of other corporate entities, such as United States retailer Target, in physical activity-based school schemes as part of *Let's Move*. Reflecting the report's encouragement for educational providers to seek greater commercial partnerships to increase resourcing and provision (in lieu of decreased state support), Target, for example, provides support for a range of physical activity, sport and leisure programmes to be operated within schools and local communities. The scheme is comparable to the involvement of grocery retailer Sainsbury's in the United Kingdom with its official sponsorship of the annual school games and a variety of programmes operated under the auspices of the Youth Sport Trust (Kohe & Chatziefstathiou, 2017; Griffiths & Armour, 2013). Although established in the United States, from its inception *Let's Move* has been international in its scope. The report's international significance can also be seen as an ability to inform, and be a model for, sport and educational policy development and actions in other contexts. In the United Kingdom, for example, *Let's Move* provided the basis and a comparative reference point for the Nike-funded Young Foundation's '*Move it*' report (2012), which, to add to the United Kingdom's growing pile of physical activity/sport-related policies of late (Evans & Davies, 2015; Houlihan, 2016), provided data and a framework for action to support broad social, cultural and industry change.

Nike has also propelled further stakeholder synergies. Foremost has been the Aspen Institute's *Project Play* initiative. Following from the *Let's Move* report (and involving Nike and many of the same stakeholders), *Project Play* (https://www.aspenprojectplay.org/project-play-2020/) was launched in 2013 and in 2015 produced the *Sport for All, Play for Life: A Playbook to Get Every Kid in the Game* (Aspen Institute, 2015). With updated empirical data and renewed strategies and initiatives, the report rehearsed many arguments set forth in *Let's Move*. Where *Let's Move* showcased the necessity of stakeholder synergies, *Project Play* focussed on establishing more selective membership comprising high-level sports organisations (e.g. the United States Olympic Committee and National Hockey League), prominent companies (e.g. Amazon, Nike, Target) and professional services (e.g. the American College of Sports Medicine and the Global Obesity Prevention Center). Rebranded in 2018 as *Project Play 2020*, the revised project entails greater efforts to track national physical activity-related metrics, develop the inspirational champions scheme (entailing celebrities working within and alongside local schools and sport providers) and make continued lobbying efforts to change policy and education priorities.

For Nike, the intentions of *Let's Move* and *Project Play* have generally been the same. Essentially, there is a moral crisis to be resolved, and schools and communities are *the* spaces to be targeted. The reports compose a scene in which youth are 'in need' and/or 'at risk', the spaces resource 'poor' and ill-equipped to deal with the severity of challenges physical inactivity entails and stakeholder intervention is not only fait accompli but a necessity. Notwithstanding Nike's intentions, *Designed to Move* is underpinned by the ideology of collective moral crises that has long-characterised physical inactivity/obesity/physical education discourse (Bell, McNaughton & Salmon, 2011; Gard, 2015; Gard & Wright, 2005). Language such as '...physical inactivity actually seems normal', 'the economic costs are unacceptable, the human costs are unforgivable', 'we must act urgently to break its deadly cycle'; '...coordinated action is urgent'; 'no one can solve this problem alone' (*Designed to Move*, 2013) is employed to stress the severity of the issue but also validates the political authority of the stakeholder consortia as a powerful voice of authority (and one with the ability to facilitate meaning and widespread global and community change). Directly with *Let's Move*, *Project Play* and *Move It*, Nike has evidenced its ability to be not just an ad hoc policy contributor and interested stakeholder but rather a policy developer and driver. Herein lies the concern.

Pragmatically, Nike operates here like many other companies in which business practice comprises activities that drive the production of both economic and ethical/social capital (Bartley & Kincaid, 2016; Knight, 2007; Rowe, Karg & Sherry, 2018). Thus, ventures into policy development (and the associated genuine concerns expressed for humanity's physical activity levels) can be understood and normalised as part of CSR. Critique of Nike on these grounds alone is warranted. However, what matters here is the degree to which Nike exists as an international policy funder, contributor, developer and implementer within the sport education sector.

Nike can evidently pull people, groups and communities together in a way that government policy work often struggles to do, and the company has garnered wide-spectrum respect for its sport and physical inactivity work. Although schools and communities, and more generally state and public-sector organisations, may possess capacities to negotiate and accommodate these sorts of global consortia, the sheer volume of resource being leveraged at the cause makes resistance difficult. Rehearsing critical pedagogues and corporate critics who have forewarned of the dangerous encroachments of the private sector in educational ideology and practice (Farahmandpur, 2006; Giroux, 2016; Golin & Campbell, 2017), Nike's policy protagonism here is problematic because it assumes that there is a natural congruity between corporate strategy, educational agendas, pedagogical practices, policy development and social philanthropy. By way of its varied reports, network formation and global permeation, Nike has driven policy discussion in political, academic and civic spheres. Not least of these spaces are schools and communities who find themselves the eventual recipient of these globalising policy frameworks and playgrounds for a perpetual parade of stakeholder initiatives, investments and interventions.

McDonalds

Whereas Nike's sport industry focus makes it a natural partner for sport and education, other corporate connections have also garnered scrutiny, one of which is the fast-food restaurant chain McDonalds. Initially established in 1940 and rebranded the McDonalds Corporation in 1955, the company has over 37,000 restaurants, holds significant sway over its competitors and accrues billions (USD) in annual revenue (Carden, Maldonado & Boyd, 2018; Lee & Lambert, 2017). Since inception, the company has operated a number of charitable ventures, including hospital support facility *Ronald McDonald House*; the *My InspirAsian* project (to celebrate Asian Americans and Asian Pacific Islanders in the United States); *365 Black* (in support of African American culture); establishing a national scholarship scheme for Tertiary study; and the universal initiatives related to promoting Science, Technology, Engineering and Mathematics (STEM) (https:// www.mcdonalds.com/us/en-us/community.html). In sport and education, McDonalds has developed a distinct identity as a 'grass-roots' partner. While sites of action have varied, McDonalds's primary remit has been to provide direct financial and practical support for a global array of projects that have impact at the local/community level. To enact its charitable mission, McDonalds has established partnerships with Tertiary education providers (namely, to enhance industry-academic synergies, provide graduate opportunities and add scholarly clout to its social development work).

Since the 1980s McDonalds's assimilation into sport spaces was afforded considerable legitimacy by its partnership with the International Olympic Committee (IOC). The company was part of the IOC's successive The Olympic Partners (TOP) programme which provided lucrative marketing rights and exposure deals for the various iterations of the Olympic Games. The arrangement enabled McDonalds to leverage its brand image within sport and, conversely, utilise sport (and particularly, endorsement of young athletes leading healthy lives) to push its corporate agendas as civic altruism. The popularity of the Olympic Games and the public appeal of McDonalds served as a powerful combination in the pursuit of capturing market spaces (in this case, youth, sport and school communities). Moreover, the partnership worked to normalise McDonalds's presence within the sector but, beyond this, position the company as 'the best choice' for schools in need of commercial sponsorship and support. Counter to this success, in 2017 the IOC decided not to renew its McDonalds partnership, with both organisations citing mutually agreeable shifts in vision, ideals and long-term strategy.

McDonalds's encroachment into young peoples' sporting lives has extended beyond the reliance on the Olympic Partnership. Under the varyingly worded ethos of 'Active lives are healthier and happier lives', for example, over the last few decades McDonalds has invested in an array of school and community sport projects. This investment has included support for Little Athletics, swimming and football leagues, equipment purchases and the provision of junior sports grants in Australia; football skills and coach education programmes, indigenous education scholarships, pedometer-based physical activity promotions in schools and partnership in Olympic education initiatives in New Zealand; development of sport based community 'McHappy' days in Brazil; supporting coach education programmes and school sport equipment distribution in South Africa; facilitating 'Youth Champions' projects that, for the 2010 Winter Olympics in Vancouver, Canada, turned young children into local reporters and quasi-brand ambassadors; and an international employee community giveback scheme (akin to Nike's *Community Impact* project). Such examples demonstrate the extent of McDonald's corporate philanthropy. In addition, however, it is evident that the company has achieved success in aligning itself with a clear health and well-being discourse.

Yet there has been notable discontent over McDonalds's associations and integration with formal curricula, school communities and youth-based educational interests. While McDonalds has invested in curricular resources and training related to business studies and professional hospitality training sector (https://www.mcdonalds.co.uk/teachers/), criticism has drawn attention to the company's exploitation of schools (e.g. with its *McTeacher* nights in which 'charitable' donations are contingent upon parent/teachers offering 'volunteer' labour in the company's restaurants) (Bakir, Blodgett & Salazar, 2017; Golin & Campbell, 2017; Marsh, 2017; Morran, 2016; Moran, Rimm & Taveras, 2017). McDonalds's educational connections have also drawn official condemnation from corporate accountability organisations (e.g. https://www.corporateaccountability.org/food/) and educational sector watchdogs (e.g. https://www.commercialfreechildhood.org/). Responding to the prevailing public malaise over the corporatisation of education (Anaf et al., 2017), and with McDonalds specifically, these organisations have lobbied strongly against the dependency relationship corporate-education partnerships create and the normalisation, and positive impressionism, of fast-food associations within school contexts. This critical response has not, however, been forthcoming elsewhere, and related appraisals of McDonalds's sport-based educational ventures remain limited (see, e.g., Houlihan & Bradbury, 2013; Carter et al., 2018).

The scope and significance of McDonalds's corporate consumption of youth sport and sport education spaces is undoubtedly global and profound. Nonetheless, while it may be easy to vilify the unhealthy nature of fast food, and the normalised assumptions between the company, excessive consumption and the conceptualisation of obesity, it is more difficult to condemn the extent of its efforts to offset this criticism by trying to improve peoples' lives, communities and sporting experiences. Moreover, the company does exist (and has shown its capacity as a 'force for good'), and schools remain in precarious position of having to judge forays into commercial partnership with issues of sustainability. Like Nike, the coalescence of thought for McDonalds's stakeholder relations emerges in shared commitments to youth, community development and public health. McDonalds distinguishes itself in that it does not seek (at least overtly and as far as evidence reveals) to be a lead policy agent or advocate within the predominant global sport and educational networks. Such a strategy might work to temper criticisms about its corporate hypocrisy, yet it does not abate a genuine concern for its pervasiveness in peoples' lives and connections to sport, physical activity and healthy lifestyles.

Coca-Cola

Other companies, such as Coca-Cola, have joined the sport education commons with vigour. Established in 1886, soft-drink company Coca-Cola has become one of the world's most recognisable brands. The business growth and global reach have been matched with effective marketing strategies that have afforded it a prominent place in consumer culture (including significant representation within sport) (https://www.coca-colacompany.com/). The company's partnerships with sport organisations and sport events are well recognised and extend from local ventures, regional and national level championships, and international mega-events. Alongside McDonalds, one of Coca-Cola's most significant relationships has been with the IOC as part of its TOP programme. While providing the company with exclusive rights and revenue within the context of the Olympic Games cycles, the partnership has also worked to legitimise the company as a committed and valued sport, physical activity, global health and educational values stakeholder (Banks, 2016; Coburn & McCafferty, 2016; Gertner & Rifkin, 2018; Powell, 2015; Powell & Gard, 2015). The company has joined the collective chorus of corporate entities now endeavouring to speak to and for youth communities, young people's sport and educational 'needs' and 'desires', and the moral 'call to action' to resolve public health woes vis-à-vis obesity and physical inactivity. Concomitantly, Coca-Cola's perpetual contributions to collective debate (backed by its legacies of community investment and scientific sponsorship) continue to afford it political capital.

Coca-Cola has demonstrated a long and involved dedication to social responsibilities in sport and education. In 1984, for example, the company launched The Coca-Cola Foundation. The Foundation's mission is to support global efforts "to share scientific expertise, practical nutrition, physical activity, and lifestyle information with consumers, health professionals and the scientific community" (https://www.coca-colacompany.com/our-company/the-coca-cola-foundation). Aligning with the company's sustainability platform, the Foundation has three priority areas: Women, water and well-being. The well-being domain focusses on education, youth development and other community and civic initiatives. In this area, Coca-Cola has engaged in initiatives that have included: the sport/educational ambassadors programme, utilising professional athletes; sponsorship of the Special Olympics and disability sport programmes; development of pedagogical resources related to raising cross-cultural awareness; creation of units and synergies with school curricula; physical activity and sport promotion community events associated with the Olympics and FIFA World Cup; participation in World Health Organisation campaigns related to healthy lifestyles and community well-being; and an 'employees-gives-back' scheme.

Coca-Cola's educational and sporting hegemony has been achieved not on its own but rather by forging direct partnerships with key stakeholders in several countries. In the United States, for instance, the company has worked with several Universities to establish scholarship funds and intern opportunities. In Argentina, long-term collaborations with non-profit, social and youth development organisations such as Cimientos have supported increases in educational participation and academic attainment. Similar efforts in China have involved the building of schools in deprived rural areas, while, in Chile, sponsorship has been given to support science and technology. More targeted school and curricula intervention has occurred elsewhere. In Egypt, for example, partnerships with the Discovery Channel and Ministry of Education have produced renewed curricula, teacher training programmes and community learning centres. Similar schemes have also been undertaken in Pakistan and the Philippines. In addition to enabling the company to accrue political, social and ethical capital, the connections have reaffirmed Coca-Cola's commitment to work within (and dominate) a particular ideological space (in this case, social responsibilities toward global health and development) (Rushton & Williams, 2011).

Coca-Cola has notable impact and reach within the sector, and, like corporate peers, possesses resource and capacity that may seem seductive and irresistible to schools, communities and young people. The economic practicalities experienced in the education and sport sectors in many countries have also necessitated that schools become accustom to accepting these commercial partnership realities (O'Reilly & Brunet, 2013). Yet, while the volume of initiatives provides evidence of the extent of its spatial occupation, such saturation also drowns out (or at least dampens) criticisms that corporate intrusions in sport and education may be ineffective, unsustainable, unhelpful, unwanted or unnecessary (Coburn & McCafferty, 2016; Edens & GIlsinian, 2005; Thorne McAlister & Ferrell, 2002). Coca-Cola's schemes may differ in context and pragmatics, yet they are united as part of Coca-Cola's altruistic corporate ideals and help the company present itself as a credible interlocutor in global debates and spaces. The issue here goes beyond *what* exactly Coca-Cola does or *why* it does it to questions about *who* it does it for, the *extent* of its operations, the *reach* of accountability and consequences, the evaluation of its obligation by youth, schools and communities (as opposed to shareholders and directors), and its power and political capacities to bend stakeholders to its causes. We pick up these concerns later. In the production section we look at Nike, McDonalds and Coca-Cola productions to showcase how this thought work transpires *in situ*.

Global – production

Nike

To recall, Nike has established its prominence as a sport and physical activity policy provider and educational sponsor through its respective *Let's Move, Move it, Action for Sport* and *Project Play* ventures. Our interest here is with the *Let's Move* report as a space of production. To start, the report contains several key parts. The first, a prelude to action that sets out the scientific and academic rationale to justify closer stakeholder collaboration and provide an impetus for greater multi-sector investments. The report proceeds by outlining a framework for action (focussing on vision: 'future generations running, jumping and kicking to reach their greatest potential'; and, two asks: 'create positive learning experiences for children' and 'integrate physical activity into everyday life'). Further sections detail how such an aim and objectives might be achieved via additional collaborations, government lobbying, national and community-level action, educational interventionism, corporate patronage and individual agency. Following 19 short case studies that highlight how aspects of the plan are already in motion, the report offers a 'new' financial funding framework (which incorporates suggestions that mix state investment, public-sector resource reallocation, corporate patronage and commercial sponsorship, volunteerism, community entrepreneurialism, outsourcing and social-funding mechanisms). Taken in totality, the report represents a wide ranging blueprint to sustain change in attitudes and actions on physical inactivity. While the report may be critiqued for its idealistic vision and universalistic approach, for the last decade it has provided a substantive resource for the sector and its stakeholders, particularly in being used as a tool to drive policy discussions, economic investments, global to local level industry activity and community initiatives that have had discernible positive impacts.

With *Designed to Move*, Nike (and its network) produced a comprehensive policy document that demonstrated how collective dialogue can be formulated and enacted tangibly across diverse landscapes. However, the campaign went much further. To aid the translation of global policy to local practice, Nike produced an array of online, digital and social media resources to be utilised by groups within and beyond its stakeholder networks. These sites simultaneously turned policy rhetoric into consumable popular language, demonstrated the breadth and depth of public crises, provided a create means to engage wider audiences and manufactured assent for its ventures among youth and local communities. The *Designed to Move* website, for example, included emotive videos, practical ideas and strategies to initiate change, materials for schools and ideas for the wider sport and physical activity domain. Videos (promoted on the website, YouTube and other forms of social media) drew upon young peoples' voices to create an affective message that could garner wide audience interest. One excerpt from the latest project, '*If I had 5 extra years to live*' (which incorporates young children verbalising their hopes, dreams, fears and aspirations with varying degrees of severity and comedic value), captures Nike's well-established penchant for emotive marketing.

> For the first time in history, this generation may die 5 years younger than their parents. Let's give them those 5 years back…'I would make medicine for the sick'; 'I would probably invent something new'; 'I would win 5 championships'; 'I would try to fix everything bad'; 'I would bring my uncle back cos I miss him very much'; 'I would get more hamsters'; 'I would probably want to go looking for dark matter'; 'I would be the boss of all the chipmunks'…
> (https://www.youtube.com/watch?v=BmOlzRQTabA)

Beyond such obvious advertising cliché, the clip also included the use of generic statements about health, physical activity and well-being that serve (and pass for) the project's scientific and academic credibility. For example,

> Increasing physical activity can increase academic achievement; active kids make healthy choices; physical activity improves self-esteem; active kids are more likely to go to college or university; active kids become future leaders; kids who are physically active become higher-earning adults.

Regardless of the veracity of these statements (and respecting that they have been produced and endorsed by organisations such the ACSM and the ICSSPE), the point is that the clip is an effective ploy in projecting Nike as not only a knowledgeable authority but also one that possesses an unwavering commitment to the immediate and future needs of global youth.

Designed to Move is complemented by another of Nike's related initiatives, the *Community Impact Project* (https://communityimpact. nike.com/). Targeted at its own workforce, and encouraging the involvement of individuals within its wider network partners, *Community Impact* aims to instil in Nike's employees a sense of social commitment.

In so doing, Nike may closely align and evidence its broader corporate social responsibilities to its labour practices and business ethics. "From the start", the website proclaims,

> community has been at the core of who we are and what we do. Harnessing the power of sport as a unifying force, we're committed to helping kids reach their greatest potential and creating more equal playing fields for all.

To these ends, *Community Impact* focusses on two key areas: 'Getting kids active' and 'Fuelling communities'. Again, the message crystallises commonly held public assumptions (e.g. kids are increasingly inactive and should be made to move) and desires (e.g. get more kids active).

> Kids aren't made to sit still, they're made to play. But today's kids are part of the least active generation in history, and all that sitting doesn't sit well with us. We know kids who move are the ones who move the needle – in the classroom, their careers and in the community. Find out how Nike is getting kids moving to unleash their potential.
>   (https://communityimpact.nike.com/#/video/Lybk_K77FWI)

Across its two key areas, *Community Impact* has been working with more than 60 global community agencies, schools, educational providers or sport and/or education specific charitable organisations. In addition to its own initiatives, the project provides support (through employee 'volunteers', financial aid, physical infrastructure, training and professional development, celebrity athlete engagement opportunities and practical resources) for organisations that include *Play International* (http://pl4y.international/fr) and the *Children Sport Foundation* (http://ak.fundsport.ru/). In recent years, the *Community Impact* fund has allocated more than USD 12 million in grants to signature programmes, community projects, school sport and physical education development, physical activity initiatives, partnership work and coach education programmes (including the International Rescue Committee, *Marathon Kids* and *Buntkickgut* – a cross-cultural football league).

Initiatives such as *Let's Move* and *Designed to Move* are good examples of how Nike – as an actor in its' own right and in concert with others within its networks – might be considered as an industry provocateur. There is an additional point to be made here. That is, examinations of Nike have revealed its power within the context of Sport-Corporate-Education intersections. However, this power is generated and effectively obfuscated not only by its market dominance, reputation and resource but also by the vast and complex network of stakeholder partnerships it forges and the immeasurable geo-temporal and spatial landscapes its work spans. Such is the state of Nike's intersectional connectivity: It has become increasingly difficult to distinguish corporate business from philanthropic venture and where precisely Nike sits within the global sport-education/development space. Such ambiguity may not be bothersome to some, but the complex networks and the persistently changing nature of involvement, investment and initiative production serve well to also cloud the transparency of partnerships and lines of governance, accountability, ownership and responsibility (Bryson, 2004; Frisby, Kikulis & Thibault, 2004; Van den Hurk & Verhoest, 2015). While it might be that Nike shares its obligations equally and openly with its partners, as discussed in Chapter 2, stakeholder relations are rarely benign or devoid of inequities in expectation, responsibility, effort and burden.

McDonalds

For McDonalds, the Sport-Education-Corporate nexus has been a fertile space of production. In 2002, for example, the company partnered within the United Kingdom's Football Association to increase grass-roots participation, club resourcing and coaching infrastructure (https://www.mcdonalds.com/gb/en-gb/football.html). In tandem with other education and sport promotion programmes, and working in close concert with schools, McDonalds became the Football Association's official community partner (Houlihan & Bradbury, 2013). Partnership between McDonalds, national football associations and local clubs and schools has produced significant results for many communities. For example, by establishing sustainable and varied competitions structures; strengthening coach development and professional accreditation pathways; improving safeguarding measures; changing participant demographics (particularly with regard to the involvement of mothers and young women in the game); providing opportunities for young people's skill acquisition and personal development; and notably, filling gaps in school sport and physical education provision and resourcing (http://www.mcdonalds.co.uk/ukhome/Sport/Football/LetsPlay/kit-scheme.html). The company's involvement, and the effectiveness of partnerships, is also kept in check by regular policy monitoring and evaluation. Criticism of the company's image and the irony of its healthy lifestyle and sport-based CSR appear to have done little to

detract from McDonalds being acknowledged as a valuable and committed contributor to sport, education and community development
(Houlihan & Bradbury, 2013). McDonalds has replicated its football
partnership scheme across the globe and extended infrastructure, resourcing, participation and training opportunities into other sports.

McDonalds's football forays have been furthered by productive ventures in school sport and Physical education. In one global initiative,
Passport to Play (established in the United States in 2005), McDonalds
worked with educational support group Kaleidoscope to produce a
Physical education-based curriculum programme. The programme
included physical activities based on sports and games from other
countries as well Social Studies and Physical education classroom resources (to teach global awareness, cultural appreciation and health
promotion values), lesson plans, Ronald McDonald visits, 'free' kit
and special gym class. Initially trialled in 96 schools in 48 different
'markets', the scheme eventually involved 31,000 United States schools.
A key part of *Passport to Play* has involved efforts to include a wider
variety of international sport cultures. McDonald's chose to include,
for example, the indigenous Māori past-time of ki-o-rahi (a team-based
invasion game) from New Zealand, as well as other traditional games
from Brazil, India, China and Australia. The project has received
positive endorsement from State education officials, Olympians and
community development providers, who have praised its utility as a
curriculum enricher and in producing engaging student experiences,
promoting play and competition, and providing needed resource investment (see https://vimeo.com/15392967). Yet, conversely, sceptics have
been wary of *Passport to Play* and see the scheme as not just attesting
to educational McDonaldisation but a more problematic unchecked
corporate encroachment (Farahmandpur, 2006; McLaren & Sandlin,
2010; Robinson, Gleddie & Shaefer, 2016). Rehearsing Scott's (2009)
concerns about venture philanthropy (see Chapter 3), critics have taken
wider umbrage at the inequity of the company's stakeholder partnerships (which places schools, particularly those that are resource poor,
are in positions where it is difficult to resist McDonalds's attractive
schemes).

Scholarly critique withstanding, such is the extent of McDonalds's
reach that it can rightly claim to have affected the lives and sporting
experiences of millions of people. While this deserves due scrutiny,
the point here is that such substantive investment over nearly three
decades, and the track record of delivering initiative, has affirmed
McDonalds as a key nexus player in the context of public health, sport
and education. Although McDonalds may not seek to directly involve

itself in policy development in the ways peers such as Nike do, it has infiltrated school spaces and curriculum development, and has become a notable educational provider. In promoting physical activity as a public 'good' (in both senses of the word), McDonalds has situated itself firmly on the 'healthy active lifestyle' commons. Such a position is further strengthened by its alignment to other 'credible' stakeholders such as the FA (and other sport organisations), educational providers and charities.

Coca-Cola

Coca-Cola's *Active Living programme* (*https://www.olympic.org/news/ coca-cola-active-living-programme*) is another example of effective Sport-Education-Corporate connectivity. *Active Living* was launched in 2003 as an exclusive collaboration between Coca-Cola and the Dutch Olympic Committee, the Koninklijke vereniging voor Lichamelijke Opvoeding (the Dutch organisation for Physical Education teachers). The initiative is designed to promote active and healthy lifestyles by way of encouraging schools, and young people aged between 12 and 19, to take part in organised sports competition (specifically, football, volleyball, basketball, netball, table tennis and athletics). While originating in the Netherlands, the project also involved targeting 20 countries (and traditionally underserved and under-represented migrant communities). By 2011, more than 150,000 students and 48 per cent of Dutch secondary schools had participated in *Active Living*, and 5,500 participated at the national finals in Amsterdam's Olympic Stadium. Both Coca-Cola and the IOC's global reach have enabled the programme to be developed, and merged with national and local initiatives, in other locations. For example, *Active Living* also compliments, and is incorporated within, the IOC's most recent *International Global Active City* programme.

The project may not be entirely novel (other stakeholder collaborations in other countries have adopted similar approaches and employed similar language in their justifications, e.g. the Youth Sport Trust and Sainsbury's School Games). However, the longevity and dissemination of *Active Living* (and derivative and associated projects) have been beneficial to Coca-Cola's international reputation as an education and sport service provider, and as a model for other companies' CSR. In one example from Guyana, Coca-Cola partnered with national food and beverage supplier, BANKS DIH Ltd, local high schools and sport organisations (https://www.coca-colacompany.com/) to increase domestic youth participation and improve local infrastructure for further sporting competition. Other market competitors have emulated

Coca-Cola's ventures. Pepsi Co., for example, financially support and actively participate in the *Play4Life* campaign, part of the United Kingdom government's *Change4Life* initiative (https://www.nhs.uk/change4life). Not unlike other examples, the *Play4Life* campaign focusses on utilising games and play to engage young people in sport and physical activity.

One further example is worth mentioning. First trialled in 2013 and capitalising on momentum generated by the London 2012 Olympic Games, in 2014 Coca-Cola launched its *ParkLives* initiative in the United Kingdom (https://www.coca-cola.co.uk/tags/parklives). Designed to be rolled out over six years, and at an approximate cost of GBP 20 million, the scheme entails the company working in partnership with local councils, schools and sport and physical activity providers in a range of towns and cities across the nation. The intention has been to create a schedule of Coca-Cola sponsored community events that inspire and motivate the public to engage in physical activity to enhance well-being (Jane & Gibson, 2017; McCartney, 2014). Utilising the 'free' availability of public space, *ParkLives* aims to encourage engagement by promoting not only the social qualities and personal health advantages to individuals and communities but also the ease of participation. As such, Coca-Cola's *ParkLives* partners have produced a broad spectrum of events that include baby-fit workshop, fitness clubs, park runs, boot camps, social running groups, Tai Chi and Zumba classes, and eco-/environmentally sensitive and focussed physical activity sessions. These ventures formally rely upon Coca-Cola's stakeholders (e.g. UK Active, Special Olympic Great Britain, Street Games, Love Parks Week and Activity Challenge).

ParkLives is annually evaluated, and the latest report undertaken by partner UK Active (2017) has produced (unsurprisingly) a favourable assessment. The report evidenced positive associations between the events held and wider public perceptions about improving and uniting communities and providing opportunities for socialisation. Although noting considerable scope for development, the report pointed to some general increases since 2013 in participation across key demographic categories (including young mothers, socio-economically deprived participants and previously physically inactive cohorts). In education terms, the positive annual reports also help reaffirm Coca-Cola's presence as a socially minded corporate policy contributor. In a more direct sense, *ParkLives* provides the company with further opportunities to become enmeshed in people lives, sport and educational spaces. While *ParkLives* operates in summer, and thus falls mostly outside regular formal school terms, promotion and recruitment, drives have still targeted schools, school networks, kids' clubs, parents' groups and sports clubs to maximise uptake. Whereas contemporary public health rhetoric in the United Kingdom and further abroad have necessitated schools demonstrate forms of vigilant health protectionism (e.g. healthy food and beverage campaigns, lunch box surveillance policies, implementing banned food lists, etc.), schools' promotion of *ParkLives* offers Coca-Cola relatively easy and unchecked entry into young peoples' lives and spaces. Veracity of evidence and claims withstanding, the report provides an indication *ParkLives* has impact and that Coca-Cola's involvement *matters* as a mechanism of facilitating sustainable social change in physical activity levels. Moreover, there is a clear recognition that *ParkLives* is more than a physical activity initiative. As the report evidences, those that engaged in *Parklives* were more likely to identify positive statements of corporate reputation. Moreover, while some participants acknowledge the company's involvement explicitly, there is "…potential to build stronger corporate perceptions toward Coca-Cola Great Britain through park lives" (UK Active, 2017, p. 17).

Global – action

These examples illustrate the extent some global organisations have gone to consolidate a place within sport education spaces. What is evident in these examples is that while there appears to be a general coalescence of collective thought pertaining to moral panics related to peoples' health, physical activity and lifestyles, strategies of corporate colonisation are considerably varied at the level of production. Regardless, it is evident that pervasive corporate entanglement in sport education has 'worked' in the sense that in some areas around the world schools, clubs, communities and people are now better resourced to learn, play and compete than they may have been previously. Corporate initiatives have also reiterated the need for sustainable multi-sector stakeholder networks that can strategically address an array of global concerns. The Sport-Education-Corporate nexus has also provided a means of private-industry interjection in public debate and policy formation. As substantive and pervasive as the global dimensions of the nexus may be, there is still notable resistance to its presence and consequences.

One of the foremost sites of resistance and activism has been in the United States. In 2000, for example, Susan Lin founded the *Campaign for a Commercial-Free Childhood* (CCFC) (https://www.commercialfreechildhood.org). With its genesis in intellectual forums in the late 1990s, the

CCFC emerged as a specific response to concerns about the increased prevalence of commercialism in young peoples' lives. The campaign draws upon expertise from academia, law, public health and medicine, children's services, management and the business sector, and local community groups and charities to provide a political voice and lobby against corporate activities (in and beyond education) that target young children. While primarily focussed on corporate activity in the United States, CCFC takes considerable interest in targeting global corporate industry initiatives. As the organisation states, the CCFC's purpose is "to end the exploitative practice of marketing to children and promote a modern childhood shaped by what's best for kids, not corporate profits". CCFC's targets, tactics and successes have been many and varied. For example: Successful protests again the Golden Marble marketing awards that endorsed child-targeted corporate campaigns; creation of the 'Screen-Free Week' initiative; lobby companies such as the National Football League- and Nintendo to cease direct connections between online/digital gaming platforms, school sponsorship promotions and direct company advertisement; removing McDonalds's presence on school report cards and the cessation of 'McTeacher' nights; preventing Disney from marketing its 'Baby genius' merchandise as educational; halting the Gates Foundation's (discussed in Chapter 5) *inBloom* youth-based data capturing venture; and, most recently, contributing to the end of the 28-year reign of the corporate mouthpiece, Channel One, in American Schools.

The advocacy of CCFC in the United States has been complemented by the Commercialism in Education Research Unit (CERU) (https://nepc.colorado.edu/ceru-home). Established in 1998 and operating under the auspices of the National Educational Policy Center at the University of Colorado, the CERU's academic research and publications have focussed on monitoring and evaluating commercial activities in public education. The unit is founded on the belief that commercial involvement in education has implications for policy and curriculum development, teacher-student relations and schools' underlying ethos and values. A key feature of the unit has been its annual report on schools' commercialising trends, which has been used to inform sector debate and challenge practices, policies and stakeholder relations. CERU's scrutiny has highlighted exponential trends and intensification in corporate activity and commercialisation within schools, the consequences to young peoples' psychological and physical well-being, the risks to privacy and data protection, and the need for greater vigilance and proactive response to corporate practices (Molnar, 2005; Molnar & Boninger, 2015). Currently, CERU provides a much-needed empirical evidence base that might inform future solutions, responses and countermeasures but might also help give credence to new forms of thinking about how the Sport-Corporate-Education nexus could and should operate.

The CCFC's and CERU's efforts have provided a mechanism to challenge mainstream corporate-education connections and practices. Nonetheless, the organisations have only had marginal influence in bringing out about change in stakeholder behaviours within the Sport-Education-Corporate-nexus. There is, however, an encouraging model to be considered. And, with the likes of such watchdogs limited (particularly at the global level), there is a place for CCFC and CERU (and their peers) to continue their work and extend their global and sector reach. While there may be mechanisms that hold some corporate stakeholders to account (e.g. policy evaluation and governance accountabilities), and, in so doing, serve as *a* means of protecting children from exploitation and harm in the general sense, these are not intended to destabilise corporate partnership or problematise ethical sensibilities. As such, more bodies like the CCFC and CERU are needed, and there may be a more direct necessity of a comparable entity that can specifically act within the sport-education context.

Conclusion

At the global level the connectivity that binds the Sport-Corporate-Education nexus has been fortified by strong multi-level and multi-sector partnerships. Over the past few decades, these bonds have been re-galvanised as corporate entities seek to simultaneously maintain market dominance and image, and further entrench themselves in spaces that legitimate and add-value to their causes (in this case, public policy domains and the sport and education sectors). The strengthening of the nexus has also been precipitated by the forces of globalisation and neo-liberalism that propel companies toward market practices that ensure their longer-term viability, sustainability and reputation. Investments into sport-education CSR, therefore, become a strategic means to these ends. While individual bodies have responded in their own ways, international evidence (including that outlined in this chapter and elsewhere in this book) suggests sport and education providers are benefiting from, and welcoming, the increased activity and connectivity the current times provide. Of concern, however, is that while there may be a strong ethos against corporate colonisation evident in the mainstream education sector (e.g. with the work of CCFC and CERU), this degree of scepticism and activism with regard to sport education has not yet gained widespread traction.

In evaluating the global aspect of the nexus, and moving forward to consider regional and local spaces, it is useful to draw attention to a few preliminary considerations. As several scholars have noted, global partnerships (particularly those in the health realm) make sense and, in these times, necessitate the acceptance of multi-stakeholder alliances for sustainability, saturation and success (Jane & Gibson, 2017; O'Reilly & Brunet, 2013; Rushton & Williams, 2011). This is, arguably, a reality. Complex and extensive stakeholder connections are not, furthermore, necessarily or inherently problematic. Indeed, public-private-third sector connections provide impetus for social innovation and change. Stakeholders are, too, already working effectively together; sharing synergies of thought, production and action that appear to be meaningful in the context of changing peoples' lives. Unity of thought has extended to unity of resources, strategies and actions in a way that has enabled partnerships to considerably increase international scope. Nonetheless, counter arguments are also compelling.

Partnerships, such as those witnessed in the nexus, present an effective means to 'fill gaps' in sectors. This might be advantageous, but it also creates and exacerbates inequities between stakeholders and may rely on some partners' vulnerability and reliance on support and aid. The ever-changing nature of connections, partnerships and networks has also created complicated landscapes, where there is often significant overlap and repetition with stakeholders' work and that of other institutions (Jane & Gibson, 2017; Frisby, Kikulis & Thibault, 2004). Overlap and matters of accountability may be one concern, yet a more pressing issue with these partnerships is with their global focus. "The problem", Williams and Rushton (2011, p. 19) note, "is that power over real people's health in other countries lies with bodies, whose constitutional origins and current operations are remote from the 'subjects' they are governing". Under this logic, the analogy of spatial colonisation we employ in this book thus makes sense. However, what is being stressed at this point is that such connections warrant further examination not because of the complexities of their existence but because they have effectively replicated and replaced extant geopolitical arrangements and power relations. What needs considering from here is the extent to which corporate stakeholders and associated partnerships may complement supra-/trans-national and domestic priorities, while not detracting, or supplanting, resource and focus from local/national agendas (Horine & Stotler, 2004; Jane & Gibson, 2017).

5 The Sport-Education-Corporate nexus
Regional cases

Introduction

As evidenced previously, nexus collaborations have involved global entities working together on enterprises that are often widely disseminated and/or comprise significant internationalising agendas. The universality of some nexus initiatives has been of value for evidencing stakeholders' abilities to contribute to global concerns and wider humanitarian causes. Namely, by reaffirming the utility of sport as a universal 'truth' and an international imperative. Yet global(ising) initiatives have received critique for not adequately synergising with the unique regional and/or local spaces they seek to inhabit (Black, 2010; Collison et al., 2017a; 2017b; Rossi & Jeanes, 2016; Schulenkorf, 2012). The concern is not that stakeholders are necessarily unaware of regional idiosyncrasies. McDonalds's football initiatives, for example, are often modified at the national or regional level to better reflect contextual specificities (e.g. using recognisable sport role models, adopting provincial vernacular and symbols, and utilising cultural referent points). Rather, the contention is that the general flux of geo-historical-political nuances can create conditions, uncertainties and tensions that may precipitate concerns for stakeholder collaborations in situ and work against the viability, impact and sustainability of collaborative sport education projects. Furthermore, the presence of multiple sport education stakeholders working on the same agendas within a specific region may inadvertently counter extant spatial priorities and community actions (Davies, 2016; Mansfield, 2014; Svensson, 2017). Moreover, the notional parameters of some regions (here we also include large entities and countries, e.g. the European Union, the United States, sub-Saharan Africa, West Africa, Middle East, Balkan or Baltic States and post-conflict regions) may complicate stakeholders' efforts to establish defined terrains of occupation.

Demarcating regional space enables stakeholder partnerships to not only consolidate resources but also develop wider recognition for their work that might also translate into increased political agency and power. Where geopolitical flux remains pronounced or amid prevailing economic downturns and turbulence, demonstrating a commitment to cross-organisational and multi-sector partnership within a region may garner organisations kudos and provides evidence of long(er)-term progress and 'meaningful' legacies and impacts. Accordingly, in this chapter we explore these ideas by drawing on three primary examples. These include: The Federation International de Football Association (FIFA) and United Nations (UN) partnerships with communities and corporate entities in Sport for Development and Peace initiatives; the International Olympic Committee (IOC) and UN Education, Scientific and Cultural Organisation (UNESCO) work within Europe; and, corporate foundations' involvements with sport education providers. Rehearsing our structural focus on thought, production and action, we take interest in how regional issues add to stakeholder relations and examine how sport and educational providers negotiate connections, activities and commercial and regional political influences within these settings.

Regional thought

FIFA

Football has long been utilised by Sport-Education-Corporate nexus stakeholders. Football's global popularity provides a social and cultural currency organisations, educationalists and corporate entities have valued and operationalised to their individual and collective means. FIFA has stood as the eminent organisation for the game and have also overseen the development of its global social responsibility and educational development activities. Not only are FIFA a dominant global actor – they hold power and influence over the regional and national federations, and spaces in which football-governing bodies, corporate entities, state agencies, professional teams and athletes, and advocate groups come together and use the sport to facilitate social or cultural change. With significant wealth, FIFA maintains control over distribution of financial resources for humanitarian causes and related decision-making and agenda setting (particularly in terms of which regions and causes are considered 'in need' and/or which development projects best reflect FIFA's philanthropic contribution to global causes) (FIFA, 2005, 2014, 2017).

FIFA's 'Football for Hope' (or Hope) programme is one area of regional connectivity that demonstrates stakeholders' unity around altruistic thought. "Through its unique power and universality", FIFA claims, "football can bring people together, transform lives and inspire entire communities. It creates powerful opportunities to break down barriers to social development, education and health awareness" (2018, n.p). To this end, the Hope programme brings together FIFA's members, the UN, UNESCO, sport for development organisations and corporate partners to sponsor, develop and promote football in socio-economically impoverished and/or geopolitically fraught regions (e.g. Sub-Saharan and West Africa, Central America and post-conflict areas of the Balkans and South-East Asia). FIFA provides opportunities for partners to come together and establish a platform for global development initiatives, peace projects and Corporate Social Responsibility (CSR) activities. FIFA are significantly well-resourced to be able to undertake its Hope programme alone. However, by forging (or forcing) coalescence among its stakeholders toward its specific 'vision' for the sport in certain global regions, FIFA consolidates its authority and legitimacy. FIFA's dominance as a lead contributor has enabled it to establish a set of philanthropic interests beyond the game around which other commercial entities can orientate their investments. In so doing, the organisation has also ensured that its own, and its corporate partners', commercial interests are recognised and privileged. In the case of the Hope programme, this has manifested at the regional level, ensuring that key corporate partners are predominant (and at times often exclusive) contributors to sport education productions (as is the case with the Football for Hope festival in Rio De Janeiro, Brazil) (FIFA, 2014).

IOC

Global yet regional connections are also evident in the IOC's sport pedagogy projects. As the world's imminent sporting organisation, the IOC controls the Olympic Games and ensures the preservation and development of the Olympic movement (an ethos and activities built around celebrating synergies of sport, culture and education). To this end, the organisation has generated its own brand of physical pedagogy (one aligned to key humanitarian/universal 'Olympic ideals' – promoted as a distinct philosophy of Olympism) (IOC, 2017). At its core, Olympism is an amalgam of virtues the IOC deems significant and that they believe lay at the heart of physical practice and global community interactions. Over time, these ideals have become entrenched within sport discourse and have also been adopted by organisations, groups and individuals throughout the sporting industry (Chatziefstathiou, 2011; IOC, 2017; Lenskyj, 2012; Naul et al., 2017). The IOC's international scope affords it an effective platform to disseminate its ideals, but the organisation's prestige and power have also enabled it to convince others of the merits of its educational mission. While over the late 20th and early 21st centuries the IOC has undertaken an array of educational initiatives, the relatively recent Olympic Values Education Project (OVEP) provides a useful example of this thought coalescence.

Established in 2010, OVEP is a consolidation of the IOC's educational projects that aims to 'mainstream Olympic values' and develop professional development and training, networking opportunities and resource support for those undertaking sport educational (or sport-related development) work (Kohe & Collison, 2019). While the IOC is sufficiently resourced, OVEP works with corporate stakeholders within The Olympic Partner (TOP) programme and a key UNESCO partnership (United Nations, 2015). Irrespective of noted tensions in its relationship with UNESCO in global education and sport-related development (Meier, 2017), the IOC-UNESCO partnership has been advantageous. Combined, the two organisations hold a significant market and influence over sport education. In addition to the IOC's global operations and those channelled through its National Olympic Committees, for example, UNESCO works in over 9,000 schools in over 180 countries (United Nations, 2015). Shared organisational ideologies have merged as the organisations have made strategic decisions to align, influence and lead governance discussions, networking and collaborations, policy development, agenda setting and evaluation and monitoring throughout the sector. A specific partnership, for example, between the IOC-UNESCO, International Council of Sport Science and Physical Education (ICSSPE), World Health Organisation (WHO), other UN agencies, charitable organisations and commercial entities has been effective in producing quality standards and guidelines for Physical Education (United Nations, 2015). The IOC has also worked with additional stakeholders who have shared similar humanitarian, development, educational and/or sporting agendas and interests. In one initiative, entitled 'Getting Coach potatoes of the couch', collaboration included partnership with the Commonwealth Secretariat, Laureaus (the 'Sport for Good' agency), the Qatar Foundation, the Swiss Academy for Development and the Marshall Plan with Africa, plus additional support offered from participating National Olympic Committees and their corporate partners.

Sport organisations, educationalists and the corporate sector may ascribe different worth to sport education and development investments, yet the sectors appear united at one level by a common belief that there are fundamental humanitarian values to defend, protect and serve (including that sport is a recognised human right and vehicle for improved/improving social citizenship) (Chatziefstathiou, 2011, 2012a, 2012b; Culpan & Wigmore, 2010; Kohe, 2010). Moreover, that there are specific groups, communities and regions that warrant dedicated focus, attention and care above others. For FIFA, the IOC and partners, humanitarian ambitions have been framed in universal terms (with collective thought manifesting itself as commitment to global 'progress', 'opportunity' and 'equality'). However, approaches to universal idealism have had to be grounded by geographic and political realities. For the IOC, this has necessitated devolving responsibilities to regional National Olympic Committee networks. These regional operations provide a means through which the IOC can work with its own stakeholders and allies (e.g. the European Commission, UN/UNESCO), and those with greater familiarity with contextual specificities (e.g. regional development, non-governmental and governmental agencies), to disseminate its ideology, invariably, more effectively and efficiently.

Corporate foundations

FIFA and the IOC's respective partnerships with the UN/UNESCO, and other organisations, are well recognised and provide a model for regional sport education operations. There are, however, further examples that help understand how collaborative regional aims, objectives and initiatives are established in the nexus. Corporate foundation collaborations are a case in point. Corporate foundations (referred to also as private philanthropic organisations) have existed for considerable time (having emerged of the back of industrialisation and colonisation activities). Yet, in recent decades, there have been notable developments in the scope of foundation activities. Of concern here are the discernible efforts some foundations have made to exert increased power and influence over regional spaces within the interrelated health, welfare, sport and education domains (Harman, 2016; Rushton & Williams, 2011). Unlike other charitable stakeholders illustrated in this book, foundation revenue typically derives not from multiple external avenues but from a distinct source (Rushton & Williams, 2011). Corporate foundations are distinct in that their financial basis is derived from private wealth (indirectly or directly accrued from business ventures) or defined corporate programmes. Changing realities and attitudes to state governance, multilateral governance and corporate involvement, scholars note, have made conditions amiable for increased foundation-led partnerships (Harman, 2016; McCoy, 2011). While foundations of varying types can be found around the world, in the United States their presence has drawn scrutiny in the context of public- and private-sector responsibilities toward health agendas (McGoey, 2015; Rushton & Williams, 2011). Two examples considered here are the Aegon Transamerica Foundation (ATF) and the Gates Foundation.

Established in 1994, the ATF (https://www.transamerica.com/individual/why-transamerica/who-we-are/aegon-transamerica-foundation/) is the philanthropic branch of the Transamerica Corporation (an Aegon subsidiary). Founded in 1928, Transamerica established its reputation within the insurance, financial services and investment sector, and funds both the ATF and the Transamerica Institute (focussing on health and retirement studies). In keeping with its corporate remit, the foundation commits to projects related to life, education and well-being. As such, ATF's activities are focussed on several investment areas, including arts and culture, civic and community, education and financial literacy, health and wellness, human services and an employee contribution scheme called United Way. ATF provides financial grants to community non-profit organisations and takes a leading role in determining a wealth of priorities and actions within the charitable and community spaces across the country. The foundation also explicitly encourages its support for key areas that have a high concentration of Transamerica employees (currently key cities in 9/50 states of the United States). In 2016 the foundation donated USD 6,898,498 to its various causes (ATF, 2016). One key area has been in promoting the intertwining of financial health with physical health/activity. The ATF's interest in sport falls across its civic, community, education and health and welfare commitments, and to these ends the foundation has forged alliances within sport organisations and education providers to enhance regional sport development and curriculum development and provision.

ATF is one of hundreds of corporate entities and foundations that makes investments into the United States' education sector and one of the many that explicitly fund health, well-being and sport programmes. In addition to sponsoring sports teams and athletes, for example, ATF has established connections with the American Heart Association, Massachusetts Institute of Technology, Professional Golf and Tennis Associations, sport-related foundations (e.g. the Zach Johnson Golf

Foundation) and regional educational providers and local schools. At a time when economic precarity and corporate malfeasance have warranted closer accountability of financial institutions, ATFs ability to fund such a wide scope of projects is of value; namely, in evidencing Transamerica's CSR obligations (Korschun, Bhattacharya & Swain, 2014). Like other corporations and their philanthropic auxiliaries, ATF also has the capacity on its own to effect positive regional impact across the United States. Yet the Foundation's individual efforts and public credibility are invariably improved when multi-sector alliances can be forged (Giulianotti, 2015; Kombe & Herman, 2017; Youde, 2013).

Unlike other corporations directly shaping sport and education, ATF works differently by operating indirectly through proxy and affiliated organisations and entities. While, for instance, it does not explicitly support primary and secondary school events, it does fund and work with partners who have this remit. In addition, ATF participates in the country's well-established match-funding programme, in which employees' contributions to local schools and charities are doubled by Foundation funds. This approach enables ATF to oversee a wide philanthropic portfolio while also ensuring that delivery mechanisms and responsibilities lay at the point of service. Such alliances support collaborative thinking (e.g. improving the population's general health and well-being) but enable resources, effort, burden and recognition to be (potentially) shared. Though its involvement may be considered less interventionist than other corporate entities, ATF is present in sport education spaces, advocating health, welfare and physical well-being discourse; ensuring that these discourses remain sector priorities and that resources are distributed to specific areas and causes; and maintaining and normalising assumptions about the advantages of corporate patronage.

By comparison, the Gates Foundation (https://www.gatesfoundation.org/, officially the Bill and Melinda Gates Foundation [BMGF]) has forged a larger sector footprint within the region. Initially formed in 1994 as the William H. Gates Foundation, the organisation was rebranded in 2000 by Bill and Melinda Gates (control of the foundation is shared by the Gates with fellow corporate icon Warren Buffett). The Gates Foundation has an annual endowment of over USD four billion, making it both the United States' and the world's largest philanthropic organisation (Harman, 2016). The Foundation's mission is to contribute to global scale change in the areas of poverty, health and education. To this end, it has established a significant presence in over 100 countries and works heavily across Europe, the Middle East, Africa, India, China and the United States. Although focussed on developing countries, the Foundation contributes approximately USD 500 million to aid within the United States. The organisation also funds an array of other global organisations, including the WHO, the United Nations International Children's Emergency Fund (UNICEF), Rotary International, tertiary institutions, international development agencies and research organisations as well as stakes in numerous large global companies. Maintaining close relations with respective United States governments, the Foundation utilises philanthropic partnership networks (e.g. links with high net worth individuals, corporate and charitable foundations, education and health providers, national and international companies, and public service organisations). Further to this, the Foundation works with philanthropic partners (such as Giving Tuesday, Markets for Good, Red Nose Day and the International Center for Not-For-Profit Law) to shape policies within the global corporate social responsibility sector.

The Foundation's collaborations, projects and general business are expansive and ever changing, with its levels of investment and interest varying across spaces. Accordingly, the Gates Foundation's reach, and the extent of its stakeholder connections and activities, is both impressive and difficult to measure. Moreover, for all the successful connections and initiatives it undertakes and reports, there are others (by its own admission) that garner scant recognition. The Foundation has, however, successfully consolidated its position as fundamental to the global and American public health knowledge economies. While not the only stakeholder, their presence, and the issues they deem as priorities, evidently matter. For the Foundation, sector collaborations are part of the pragmatics of business and progress. "We work with companies like GSK and Johnson & Johnson because they can do things no one else can", Melinda Gates (Gates Foundation, 2018) proclaims,

> Every partner we work with is required to make products developed with foundation funding widely available at an affordable price. Ideally, we'd like companies to seek our more opportunities to meet the needs of people in developing countries.

There is evident recognition here that it is relatively easy to bend partners to certain ideas and missions. "World leaders tend to take our phone calls and seriously consider what we have to say", Melinda acknowledges, "Cash-strapped school districts are more likely to divert money and talent toward ideas they think we will fund" (Gates Foundation, 2018). Stakeholder partnerships here are conceptualised and materialised in hard economic terms. "We think poor people should benefit from the same kind of innovation in health and agriculture that has improved life in the richest parts of the world", Bill Gates adds:

> Much of that innovation comes out of the private sector. But companies have to make a return on their investments, which means they have little incentive to work on problems that mainly affect the world's poorest people. We're trying to change that—to encourage companies to focus a bit of their expertise on the problems of the poor without asking them to lose money along the way.
> (Gates Foundation, 2018)

The point here is not whether the Gates Foundation's investments are genuine and advantageous, or otherwise, but rather considering how the position has emerged, garnered legitimacy and been sustained.

Regional production

FIFA

As mentioned earlier, the Hope programme affords FIFA means to bring a wide array of stakeholders together. Extending this commitment beyond thought space, FIFA have formalised connectivity through its partnership strategy and marketing activity. As FIFA's 2005 report '*Make the World a Better Place: Football for Hope*' notes, partner networks are necessary for the effective implementation of programmes and joint advancement of human development. Collaboration is, for FIFA, an imperative of production. Yet within collaborations there are specific relationships and connections that are of greater value. Foremost of which are FIFA's relationships within its corporate partners (e.g. VISA, Coca-Cola, Adidas, Sony, Emirates and Hyundai). FIFA's corporate partners feature not only as primary sponsors of sport education and development programmes but have marketing prominence within initiatives. The breadth and reach of the Hope programme, FIFA recognise, have made it an attractive site for public- and private-sector investment (FIFA, 2017, 2018). Of most significance is that FIFA's programme provides a global platform and a variety of regional spaces for corporate partners to demonstrate their social responsibility, specifically, commitments to civic development, humanitarian aid and community development.

Pragmatically, FIFA's approach makes sense. The connections forged capitalise on FIFA's substantive resources and networks, and those of other stakeholders who share its ideals to enact change where it is considered needed most. Moreover, the collaborations mean FIFA can establish itself as a central hub and authority for global football development activity. Such collaboration may offer a sensible, and invariably ethical, approach to development and education (e.g. in countering critiques of Global North privilege and dominance). However, the programme is still contingent on a set of power relations that are underscored by corporate imperatives. To facilitate the spread of the Hope programme, for example, FIFA have created a collaborative (yet still hierarchical) management and delivery structure that uses regional and local practitioners and organisations. Such a system ensures entities remain reliant on the patronage, visibility and economic support afforded by the organisation and its corporate partnerships. Although the actual processes of production entail negotiation and management as lines of responsibility and resourcing are worked out and operationalised, FIFA's sport education projects go relatively unchallenged by their partners. In addition, the complexities of its networks also obfuscate efforts to apportion direct responsibility and ownership to the parent organisation when initiatives may not meet desired regional or local outcomes envisioned by FIFA or its collaborators (Collison et al., 2017a, 2017b; Darnell, 2010). As explored shortly, there are contestations to FIFA's occupation of football development spaces. Yet, for the most part, the organisation retains its position as *the* gatekeeper for legitimising sector work and participation therein.

IOC

The IOC's (and UNESCO's) collaborative work has also been undertaken in concert with a 'family' of commercial partners. Typically, the IOC collaborates with companies within its official The Olympic Partner (TOP) programme. These companies have included Coca-Cola; Bridgestone; Atos; Dow; General Electric; Omega; Panasonic; Proctor & Gamble; Samsung; Visa; and, until recently, McDonalds. These partnerships enable the IOC to produce a wider variety of pedagogical initiatives and outreach work. Commercial collaborations have also helped ensure productions have the desired consumer reach. With OVEP, for example, the IOC partnered with International Sport Multimedia Limited (ISML), an international entertainment software company. As the IOC's official software licensee, ISML has an established reputation for digital content provision within the sport sector. Having developed marketing and advertising campaigns for the organisation and many of the IOC's TOP partners, ISML's expertise has been valuable in marketing OVEP successfully at regional and local levels. ISML generated digital content, video and gaming resources, and electronic marketing campaigns (utilising connections with SEGA, Panasonic, Ubisoft and YouTube) to promote the OVEP and provide mechanisms NOCs and stakeholders could use in their own dissemination.

The IOC's use of its TOP partners and ISML in the production of OVEP reflects contemporary practices within the Sport-Education-Corporate nexus whereby stakeholders share a remit to broaden their appeal to wider audiences (in this case youth markets) and work of capitalising their respective and collective market shares (Davies & Bansel, 2007; Gulson, 2008). The connectivity has established a financial basis to ensure OVEP's sustainability and created practical platforms upon which the IOC and partners can spread shared values. ISML's role, in this regard, has been integral in ensuring that there is a degree of coalescence between the IOC's and corporate partners' sport education-related digital content and youth engagement/marketing strategies. OVEP is integrated with already existing content on the IOC's website (www.olympic.org) and is cross-referenced (or hyperlinked) with corporate partners' corresponding websites and/or digital promotion campaigns. Collaboration has also been advantageous for the IOC in utilising sponsors' existing markets and popularities to win-over new audiences to the IOC's brand and values. In the United Kingdom, for example, the IOC-Coca-Cola partnership enabled the latter to create a youth-orientated marketing campaign, leveraging regional spaces associated with the London 2012 Olympic Games. Framed as a 'business studies' challenge, Coca-Cola's education effectively turned students into quasi-corporate ambassadors for the company's Olympic-related network activity. The outcome for participants, in addition to academic credit, was to instil the Olympic family ideals of altruism, commitment to global citizenry and social investment (Coburn & McCafferty, 2016; IOC, 2017).

Corporate foundations

Foundation-led partnerships exhibit similar production qualities and raise comparable concerns. The Gates Foundation and ATF, for example, have had little difficulty in establishing specific sport and educational causes and producing tangible connections to places and communities. For these foundations, sport-related investment has helped to fulfil moral and ethical imperatives, increase commercial presence and business expansion, and enhance stakeholder networking and capacity building (Batty, 2016; Bridoux & Stoelhurst, 2014; Frisby, Kikulis & Thibault, 2004). For ATF, collaborations with several key sport and education stakeholders have been constructed to target community and/or global needs. Since 2004, Aegon and ATF have partnered with the Right to Play organisation to fund sport development (and peace) initiatives in Africa and China. Productions have included sport and play projects within socio-economically impoverished communities and sport, physical activity health and well-being programmes. These initiatives have also been aligned with ATF's community support efforts in the United States. In the United States, the ATF concentrates investment into a few key areas (https://www.aegon.com/investors/News/News/Archive/Clear-focus-for-Aegon-sponsorships/), one of which has been the direct and indirect sponsorship of educational and athletic pathway development for tennis and golf athletes. In addition to individual professional athlete sponsorship, the ATF's financial support has been used to establish and sustain junior/amateur playing facilities, and competition structures that have enabled participation and improved opportunities for young people to have positive sporting experiences and help maintain healthy lifestyle behaviours. Such collaborations have been aided by the Foundation's and organisation's shared ideological interests (couched as community/social 'responsibilities') in promoting physical activity engagement to wider populations. The ATF sponsorship and work with the Zach Johnson Foundation further enable it to meet these ends.

Created and named after renown American golfer, the Zach Johnson Foundation aims to improve individual's and community's quality of life, education and well-being using the mechanism of sport and education. The ATF and Zach Johnson alliance works in concert with schools, youth support groups and community agencies to create educational support and training opportunities for young people and their families. Based in Iowa, the *Kids on Course* initiative, for example, focusses on closing existing inequalities of opportunity in the American educational sector by implementing pedagogical interventions that improve young people's personal and professional skill sets, and smoothing potential transitions into higher education. To note, similar efforts were seen in the United Kingdom, where, post-London 2012 Olympic Games and amidst sport legacy funding concerns and developments (Kohe & Chatziefstathiou, 2017), Aegon partnered with the Lawn Tennis Association to develop school tennis programmes. Stakeholder connectivity here provided a means by which schools could mobilise newly generated State funding, sport organisations could rejuvenate participation numbers and club interest, and corporate entities could easily demonstrate civic altruism and maintain public presence (LTA, 2013; Tennis Foundation, 2018).

In contrast to the ATF's work, the Gates Foundation's productions have been more pronounced. Notwithstanding the attention the Foundation has received for directing global health policies (Barkan, 2011; Harman, 2016; McGoey, 2015; Youde, 2013), its investments in education spaces (particularly with the United States) are also notable. One example is the Foundation's partnership with *SHAPE* – The American Society for Health and Physical Educators (https://www.shapeamerica.org/). SHAPE is the leading national organisation for professionals in the sector and provides a disciplinary home, resource support, professional development and networking opportunities for its members. In addition, the organisation is the lead entity for formulating State-wide policy and subject-related pedagogical directions. In 2015 the organisation developed the '*50 Million Strong*' campaign, which aimed to increase young people's engagement and long-term participation in sport, physical activity and healthy lifestyle behaviours (https://50million.shapeamerica.org/about-us/; SHAPE America, 2016). Recently, SHAPE established an agenda toward 2029 that targets four key areas: Physical activity, healthy behaviours, positive Health and Physical Education policies, and National Health and Physical Standards. The aim is to mobilise some 50 million young people toward sustainable health and physical literacy pathways. The agenda builds on United States department guidelines and international recommendations set by organisations such as the WHO, IOC and UN. Foundation funds have also been channelled into other education areas, including: Support for early learning, post-secondary and high schools; enhancing teaching quality and student experience; school district partnerships for professional development; and funding research think tanks and boards responsible for the development of new policies and financial frameworks (McCoy & McGoey, 2011; McKeown-Moak, 2013). In the United States, the Foundation has involved itself in sport education through the endowment of university chairs, partnering with educational innovation organisations, contributing to Sport Relief and related charitable appeals, supporting pedagogical and training partnerships with football and youth clubs, and funding the global policy and advocacy organisation Beyond Sport foundation (http://www.beyondsport.org/; Barkan, 2011; Castro-Martinez & Jackson, 2015; Harman, 2016; Hayhurst, 2011; McGoey, 2015).

In some areas Gates Foundation contributions are neither direct nor explicit, and it may appear that its interest in sport is tenuous. The Gates Foundation, for example, neither commissioned the *50 Million Strong* campaign nor published the guiding document (in contrast to Nike, which plays a direct role in policy production). A moot point perhaps, however, the invariable mobilisation and effectiveness of the campaign required substantive financial and organisational resourcing (e.g. at the grass-roots delivery end to enact initiative development and implementation, and at the upper level to aid advocacy and political lobbying). The campaign's underlying empirical studies were also funded by the Foundation (SHAPE America, 2016). What is evident, however, is that the Foundation possesses means within sport education spaces to use capital (e.g. grants, research funding, networking abilities and political clout) to mobilise relevant actors within the sector to take up individual and collective actions in priority areas. Such areas may already be a part of stakeholders' existing remits and operations, but the Gates Foundation is *the* most well-resourced to support and sustain energies being spent toward particular ideals and initiatives. Reflecting wider corporate trends in the sector, the Foundation's expansions into educational political spaces is now firmly entrenched and unlikely to abate anytime soon (Reckhow & Snyder, 2014). The Foundation, Harman contends, "occupies a position of authority in global health governance through its ability to use private wealth to buy influence in the policies and priorities of international institutions and shape the knowledge and ideas that underpin global health policy" (2016, 352). Like Nike (see Chapter 4), such involvement makes it possible to consider foundations within the construct of a shadow state and as a clear contributor as a policy developer and lobbyist with the sport education sector (Levermore & Moore, 2015; Piggin, 2015).

Regional action

To recall, our conceptualisation of action (outlined in Chapter 2) is based on taking produced meanings and resources (e.g. FIFA's Hope programme, the IOC's OVEP or the Gates Foundation's *50 Million Strong* campaign) and operationalising them in ways that might resonate in specific contexts. While many productions are grand in scale and may be designed to work at the universal/global level, ultimately there are degrees of translation, transformation and reconfiguration that occur at the regional (and local) levels as stakeholders negotiate and adapt knowledge and meanings to align more closely with in situ ideal and practices. Recognising these difficulties, Bill Gates notes of the Gates Foundation that "it's not so much a question about what we do, but how we do it. Do we really understand people's needs? Are we working with people on the ground?" (Gates, 2018). "We're acutely aware", Melinda Gates acknowledges similarly,

> that some development programs in the past were led by people who assumed they knew better than the people they were

trying to help. We've learned over the years that listening and understanding people's needs from their perspective is not only more respectful—it's also more effective.

(Gates, 2018)

With FIFA and IOC initiatives, too, regional action is often first witnessed in the transmission of power and responsibility for governance and delivery to regional organisations that, while less financially equipped or resourced, possess networks, infrastructure, community understandings and established organisational routes/roots that may be of value. Yet action is rarely straightforward and can often comprise risk and necessitate innovation and creativity as organisations and stakeholders work to ensure a 'best fit' (if such a fit exists) between the producer, the production and the consumer. While at times action may generate positive outcomes and opportunities for stakeholders, it can also cause antagonisms that work against collective determinism.

For FIFA and the IOC, their extensive actions have involved a wide array of stakeholders (far beyond those identified in this book). The 'messiness' of players also makes understanding the nature and scope of action with these organisations difficult to identify and evaluate. Between 2005 and 2015 the 'Football for Hope' campaign, for example, sponsored approximately 170 NGOs in 78 countries to run over 450 programmes. Central to the effectiveness of the Hope programme was FIFA's ability to utilise regional companies, organisations and facilitators to provide specialised knowledge pertinent to regional idiosyncrasies. UNICEF, for example, was one such organisation that – with its well-established presence in socio-economically deprived regions, existing regional centres and networks with local organisations, businesses and sport and education providers – was best placed to advise FIFA on how and where its funding might best be directed. Subsequently, the imperatives and resources of the Hope programme could then be taken up by appropriate regional representatives and/or local organisations. Either considered a design feature or borne out of management necessity, FIFA's 'hands-off' approach provides a means by which a sense of cultural appropriateness (and to a lesser extent, ownership) might be fostered. Moreover, with FIFA and its corporate partners operating at a distance (yet with still a visible market, branding and advertising presence) power shifts can potentially be configured that create alternative opportunities for individuals and communities to use football in ways that are meaningful to them and the spaces they inhabit. Such power transitions are, of course, fragile and perceptual, and the extent to which actions are made 'meaningful', let alone viable and sustainable, remains fallible. As scholars have long criticised, issues of ownership and control at the lower levels of the hierarchy can be considered largely illusory when large-scale organisations and sport bodies still hold sway over the political control of resources, funding, occupation and decision-making (Kay, 2010; Nicholls, Giles & Sethna, 2011).

With regard to the IOC, politics of action is similarly complex. The IOC's collaborations with UNESCO, Coca-Cola and ISML, for example, evidence how large-scale corporate agendas can form around collective ideals and be mobilised effectively within regions. The collective work done in the IOC's name has created a distinctive ideological practice (e.g. the promotion of a universal sport orientated humanitarianism) and corporate connections that are now, largely, fait accompli. Nonetheless, within the IOC's existing programmes, including the OVEP, there exist opportunities for challenging Sport-Education-Corporate hegemonies. One example has been with the Olympic education web-resource *Get Set*. Initially designed to support the '*Inspire a Generation*' agendas of the London 2012 Olympic and Paralympic Games, and now repurposed to support other sport mega event educational projects, *Get Set* encourages interested parties (namely schools and sport clubs) to utilise educational material to promote sport, physical activity, cultural/global awareness and the Olympic values (http://getset.co.uk/). Substantive parts of the website are also closely aligned with the United Kingdom's formal educational curricula. Now owned by the British Olympic Association and British Paralympic Association, *Get Set* comprises a wealth of information for practitioners and young people to use in practising and understanding sport and social responsibility in their daily lives. While those wishing to utilise the resource within and beyond the United Kingdom may still need to 'translate' or repurpose the contents, many of the resources are publicly accessible and provide a reasonable template for sport education work. Yet, in keeping with the strict marketing, licensing and copyright policies entertained by the IOC and its NOCs, *Get Set* remains a controlled platform with some content requiring formal registration and strict rules surrounding use and site access.

In contrast to *Get Set,* the *Kent 20in2012* project offered a more regionally nuanced and sensitive (re)contextualisation of Olympic-related sport education. Based in the English county of Kent, and like *Get Set* run in conjunction with the London 2012 Olympic and Paralympic Games, the initiative involved the regional county council working with local schools, service providers, a higher education institute, educational and arts charities to support (initially) 12 learning projects congruent with the aforementioned '*Inspire a Generation*' agendas (Kohe & Chatziefstathiou, 2017). Although *Kent 20in2012* drew upon many aspects of *Get Set*, the distinction was in the initiatives' regional focus on knowledge production and ownership. To this end, schools utilised Olympic-related resources as they desired, with the emphasis placed on the production of new meanings, experiences and opportunities that could promote leadership and civic participation. In this way, actions were not controlled by IOC (or NOC) (as in the case with the OVEP) and were free from corporate affiliation. Rather than rely on the IOC charter and philosophy, *Kent 20in2012* privileged local voices (in this case, young people and community advocates and activists) who were best placed to speak to and for the varied concerns and community types of the region. In keeping with the ethos of democratising pedagogy, the site operated as an open-access repository and is now maintained on an ad hoc basis.

Conclusion

The examples evidenced here demonstrate how, at the regional level, some sport industry constituents have coalesced thought toward individual and collective political agendas and ends. Beyond the efforts of familiar Sport-Education-Corporate stakeholders, the chapter also highlights some of the ways philanthropic foundations are undertaking substantive work in many regions of the world. Where FIFA and the IOC's interventions have been significantly documented and critiqued, the extent to which foundations operate within the Sport-Education-Corporate nexus is less well known. Either as part of recognised corporate establishments (e.g. the Gates or Transamerica Foundations) or as entities in their own rights, foundations have demonstrated a means and capacity to contribute to the global development and regional dissemination of sport-education projects. Both the ATF and Gates Foundation works have been of value in alleviating deficiencies in provision and resourcing, generating new knowledge and expertise, and supporting personnel and research in specific areas (some of which may not be targeted as part of state, multilateral or charitable endeavours). Yet foundation work has received criticism within health and education sectors (Harman, 2016). As such, there remains scope to examine its varied roles and positions within the sport industry's intricate networks and social development actions. We return to these ideas in the book's conclusion.

For the most part, the nexus is built around the formation of clear and strong bonds between constituent stakeholders. Yet such connections are not fixed but can be eroded within the thought, production or action spaces as stakeholders negotiate positions, enact power and mobilise resources to achieve their desired aims. For the most part, as described in the IOC, FIFA and foundation examples, there are extant hegemonies that exist that privilege the legitimacy of the/a 'lead' organisation over other collaborators. Although this may work in principle, such legitimacy is heavily contingent upon the authority afforded to the organisation by its partners in enterprise. In this case, while the IOC, FIFA and foundations wield specific power and resource, in the sport education domain their positions of authority are venerated because of the co-dependence and mutual advantage that accrues to other participating stakeholders. Educational providers, for example, gain funding, resource support and networking opportunities, whereas corporations are afforded brand exposure and capital under the guise of social responsibility and civic philanthropy.

At the global level (see Chapter 4), synergies of thought, production and action assume a universal significance (e.g. the pursuit of global health and physical activity goals). There are echoes of this at the regional levels explored in this chapter. At the regional level, however, what becomes clearer is that disruption to the centrality of global stakeholders can present new opportunities for challenging the existing status quo and provide space for confrontations to prevailing knowledge ownership. This juncture, in which regional contestations can be seen, provides a means of understanding how the sorts of reconfigurations of education (especially those that hold organisational and corporate interventionism to account) envisioned by critical pedagogues might be entertained and encouraged. We take these ideas regarding specificity and contextual nuance forward in the next chapter in our discussion of the localisation of the Sport-Education-Corporate nexus.

6 The Sport-Education-Corporate nexus

Local cases

Introduction

Throughout this book we have demonstrated the complex and contested nature of advocating, forming and negotiating nexus collaborations. The spaces of thought, production and action are often embroiled with both passive and active power dynamics that are central to the process of imagining and instigating change 'on the ground' and achieving corporate and educational goals. As articulated in Chapters 2 and 3, the notion of power acts as the consistent yet fluid force which shapes and steers the relationship building and programme forming outcomes of the nexus (Batty, 2016; Darnell, 2010). Within the nexus power is enacted in top-down, bottom-up behaviours and practices, and is evidenced in shifts in the custodial position adopted by various actors and stakeholders throughout the nexus. The manifestation of power at the local level in sport education and development initiatives has been well documented (Darnell, 2010; Jansson & Koch, 2017; Kivisto, 2016; Maguire, 2011). Building on this work, this chapter considers the transference of power and objectives and ideals experienced and exercised within the local context of corporate sponsored sport education programming. Whilst local organisations and partners are often at the mercy of corporate funding and can be seen jostling and working hard to establish a position within the nexus it is at the stage of action when power from the ground up can and should be realised.

A significant increase in educational priorities in the Global South, and, to a lesser extent, the Global North, is primarily due to a response to reformed global development goals and enhanced Corporate Social Responsibility (CSR) agendas and corporate pressures to realise civil responsibilities (Banda & Gultresa, 2015; Jules, 2017; Thorpe, Hayhurst & Chawansky, 2018). Such processes have seen the role of sport as an educational tool shaping multiple international, regional and local professional and development sectors. The final destination of local programming and impact provides an opportunity for individuals and organisations to explore and act upon their sociological imaginations (in essence, the ability to critically reflect one's lives and worlds, understand personal and collective positionality, and conceive creative and empowering futures) and encultured experiences to influence meaningful curriculums and valuable change. In addition, it is at this juncture that there may, we believe, also be possibilities to evoke elements of a meaningful critical pedagogy, namely equalities of opportunity, justice, empathy, compassion and an ethics of care (to be discussed further in Chapter 7) (Boler & Zemblas, 2003; Burbules & Berk, 1999; Freire, 2001; Giroux, 2016). Sport is often referred to in the context of local histories and is called upon to evidence and demonstrate indigenous practices, colonial histories and indigenous knowledge systems. Whilst this is important to both the consideration and appropriateness of sport as an educational tool it is also significant when realising the power dynamics at play away from the corporate and advocacy spaces often physically distant and removed from localised realities (Collison et al., 2017b; Hayhurst, 2011; Mansfield, 2014). Yet from the outset it is possible to argue that local populations and groups have often reshaped and altered foreign influences in ways to best suit and fit their own needs, preferences and cultural systems.

From the point of intervention, the local ownership of the nexus allows individuals and groups at the domestic level to utilise their ideals and values in the governance and leadership of educational programmes (Goodwin et al., 2017; Schulenkorf, 2012). Although transnational partners and global corporate funders often begin with their own agendas and ideas central to solving other people's problems, this is formulated in the absence of the local-turn (Mac Ginty & Richmond, 2013). In synergy with the work of Batty (2016), Jansson and Koch (2017), Lindsey et al. (2017), Mac Ginty and Richmond critically examined the lack of local voice and influence during the decision-making processes dominated by 'Western Bubbles' and 'Northern Rationalities'. Whilst we do not disagree with this assessment, we pay attention to the local-turn exercised beyond this space and recognise the local assertion of power, skill and knowledge at the point of implementation. Formal discourse and the politics of corporate agendas and development goals often mask the realities and importance of communities identifying and defining problems within their own spaces (Mwaanga & Mwansa, 2013; Powell, 2015, 2018; Press & Woodrow, 2005). Resolution and deciding meaningful and appropriate mechanisms for change is the last point of the nexus;

the distinction between thought, production and action is the realisation of local agendas and their ability to incite action.

Also of interest here is that the action phase exposes both the temporal and the spatial characteristics of power evident within the Sport-Education-Corporate nexus: For example, the contemporary geopolitical context and crises 'moments' that compel stakeholders to come together in certain locales and the distinct qualities of certain spaces (e.g. socio-economic, demographic, historic or cultural provenance, or nostalgic affiliation to stakeholder's agendas) (Ford, 2016; Martin et al., 2016; Müller, 2015). Scholars have also noted how stakeholder collaborations, and specifically the capacity of domestically situated groups to have agency (and, relatedly, take action), are contingent on capacities organisations/partnerships have to take advantage of specific confluences of time and space (Banda & Gultresa, 2015; Castro-Martinez & Jackson, 2015; Lindsey & Grattan, 2012; Nicholls, Giles & Sethna, 2011). Importantly, it is the physical coming together of monetary capital, freedom from corporate negotiation and social capital enabled in local spaces that constructs local ownership and power to reshape and act (Lindsey, 2013; Mac Ginty & Richmond, 2013; Mills, 2010; Peck & Tickell, 2002). What matters here is recognising within the nexus that local knowledge, cultural norms and social systems can (and already do) dictate the intricate workings of sport for education initiatives, and this often begins with the reappropriation of ideas and resources. In the following vignettes, we consider how spaces of action can be fostered and prevailing organisational nexus hegemonies challenged by creative educational enterprise.

Coca-Cola

Establishing local partnerships and engagement, and enacting local agendas come in many diverse forms. From allocating funds for programming and building resources and infrastructure to local buy-in schemes to partnership programmes intending to resource local non-governmental organisation (NGO) activities, the models of CSR and implementation has little regulation or governance to steer the format (Lindsey et al., 2017; Smillie et al., 2013; Sotiriadou, 2009). Another example that illustrates this involves Coca-Cola and its philosophy to implement physical activity programmes in every country in which it does business. While aspects of Coca-Cola global status and interventionism were considered in Chapter 4, this section acknowledges the company's local resonance. At the outset, Coca-Cola's programme "intends to reach the 200-plus countries that the company serves, including those without an actual physical presence by the company or its bottlers. Currently, Coca-Cola supports over 330 programs in 112 markets across the world" (https://www.coca-colacompany.com/stories/my-internship-with-coca-cola-promoting-physically-active-lifestyles-in-the-caribbean). Coca-Cola also endorses an internship partnership with Georgetown University's Global Human Development (GHD) programme. Each summer, two Master's candidates in the GHD programme work in Coca-Cola's offices around the world to experience first-hand their CSR strategy. Here, local NGOs were funded to implement hour-long physical education sessions for young people, and invest in research and technical skill development from postgraduate students (whilst simultaneously providing them with industry-specific opportunities to learn about the organisation's CSR agenda).

Consistent with all implementation approaches there is a need to evidence action and this form of CSR is no different. One intern's report of experiencing Coca-Cola's programme in the Caribbean and Costa Rica described the learning to be had when considering the role of business in education and local development. The intern claims that "organizations with complementary capabilities are critical for delivering effective programs" (ibid.). Such insights are valuable; even with the absence of a critical lens, this confirms that the selection of local partners is crucial to enact a corporate agenda. The assessment here reflects comparable criticism of the company that highlights the strategic political positioning of Coca-Cola as a sport, education and health advocate; the use of philanthropic power to influence decision-making; and the normalisation of stakeholder arrangements within the sector (see, e.g. Gertner & Rifkin, 2018; McCartney, 2014; Powell & Gard, 2015; Powell, 2018). Without established capacity large global brands often shy away from supporting organisations that have a limited portfolio of action or tangible outputs. The idea of the 'local' therefore is layered and presents complexities within this space and competitiveness at the grass-roots level. Implementation with a hands-off approach could be considered more attainable if working with established and already active organisations; this leaves little space for community-based projects operating within the limitations of local resources and support.

Streetfootballworld

In contrast to Coca-Cola, *Streetfootballworld* stands as the facilitator between a significant number of global corporate and sport stakeholders, most notably FIFA, Union of European Football Associations

(UEFA), Charities Aid Foundation (CAF), FedEx, Coca-Cola, Sony and local partner organisations. Established by PhD student Jürgen Griesbeck in 2002 in response to sustained levels of local conflict in Colombian communities, *Streetfootballworld* has developed into a global enterprise with a network of over 100 community organisations. With the aim of using the social cohesion and spatial familiarities football provides, *Streetfootballworld* aims to use the sport to unify community groups (particularly in locales where there is conflict, disharmony, tension and violence). To these ends, their primary role is to identify and work with local organisations to build local facilities and allocate funds for educational programming. According to their promotional material their projects "place a strong emphasis on local ownership, striving to include community members throughout the planning, construction and maintenance phases. They also present a powerful brand-building opportunity for partners looking to connect with fans in hard-to-reach communities" (Streetfootballworld, 2018, https://www.streetfootballworld.org/what-we-do/infrastructure). Such a statement demonstrates an awareness of the importance of local ownership whilst fulfilling and satisfying the needs funding organisations. Reiterating concerns expressed about locally orientated football education programmes (Castro-Martinez & Jackson, 2015; Jenkins & James, 2012; Martin et al., 2016), it is possible to question here how local capacity can truly be exercised under these conditions.

Nonetheless, in 2010 FIFA declared that part of the legacy of the South African World Cup would be the opening of 20 Football for Hope centres in 15 African nations (https://www.streetfootballworld. org/project/20-centres-2010-0). In collaboration with *Streetfootballworld* and local NGOs football centres were constructed, financed by FIFA and facilitated by *Streetfootballworld*, leaving local groups to utilise their new community facility and manage educational programmes. The physical branding of the centres is consistent; these were FIFA-financed centres, but the idea of local ownership, management, programming and educational themed priorities were left to the local partners. The important obligation or tangible exchange from the local side comes in the form of success stories, witness statements and imagery to evidence impact and value. Not unlike corporate behaviours in other sport and education domains (Bakir, Blodgett & Salazar, 2017; Jane & Gibson, 2017; Powell, 2018; Press & Woodrow, 2005), little attention, it seems, is given to the intricate educational curriculums, programme content or local engagement procedures with the community site. In this sense, the power is handed over, the FIFA legacy remains through branding, but ownership is protected by the hands-off approach that comes with facility development versus programme direction.

Unlike the evaluations offered of other flagship football and community sport development projects (Harris & Houlihan, 2016; Houlihan & Bradbury, 2013), with this model of exchange the adherence to promoting and delivering educational opportunities and programmes is difficult to quantify in terms of quality, impact and priority. Social development, community cohesion, vocational training, empowerment and physical education remains the tag line for these facilities and the stories that emerge on partner websites; however the game itself and football development inevitably occupy a large space in the everyday realities and use of these centres. As such, the risk of direct power transfer maybe the dilution of educational outcomes. For example, while local ownership and agency here is given at the cost of branding, this can be recognised as a key strategic component of playing the corporate game (for similar assessments in other contexts see Banda & Gultresa, 2015; Castro-Martinez & Jackson, 2015; Hayhurst, 2011; Hayhurst, Wilson & Frisby, 2011). In this sense corporations may also need to surrender to a hands-off approach with the arrangement of token updates to prove value. This may seem reasonable, but can anyone own something which is designed to promote other's good work? Moreover, can corporations legitimately claim impact and quality in the absence of systematic, sustained and effective educational support or evaluation beyond token imagery and selective narratives? Such questions are of value in further examination of local nexus arrangements.

Local assistance versus corporate agendas

The primary obstacle for many local NGOs and community schools is inadequate resources and equipment. Beyond the complexities of constructing and delivering appropriate curricula and meaningful content the use of sport as an effective learning tool requires materials. As also discussed in Chapter 5 in relation to philanthropic foundations, corporations have identified this need and embedded this as one possible CSR strategy. One example that gained national criticism in 2003 was confectionary manufacturer Cadbury's launch of a token-based £9mill campaign whereby young people were encouraged to consume merchandise in exchange for the opportunity to win sports equipment for their school.

> Under the 'sports4school' scheme, a school has to collect a minimum of 750 tokens before it can gain the first bit of equipment. With 2,000 tokens, all the equipment is obtained. Many schools

are likely to leap at the chance, as budgets for gyms have been slashed in recent years, and there are fewer playing fields for the traditional sports.

https://www.theguardian.com/politics/
2003/mar/30/schoolsports.schools

Not unlike other corporations, this incentive driven campaign was endorsed by the government and several high-profile athletes who backed the *Get Active* programme. The media and health experts widely condemned the campaign as an unethical marketing ploy, feeding into inaccurate messages that enhanced activity levels are more important than prescribing to a healthy diet. Lessons needed to be taken from this campaign both to reimagine the educational goals of these campaigns and to improve corporate-public relations and image. For local populations to invest in such campaigns a more considered and rounded approach was needed.

There have been, to note, efforts more recently by corporations to consider more ethical, holistic and sustainable engagements with sport, education, physical activity and health. Most recently, United Kingdom grocery company Sainsbury's has adopted a comprehensive 'Active Kids' reward scheme. Considering healthy lifestyle, diet and physical activity this campaign seeks to remove expert criticism whilst promoting their health-conscious brands of food, educational tool kits and training schemes. Their 2017 report includes the voices of experts, sports ambassadors and local populations to examine key issues, expose the challenges and suggest Sainsbury's endorsed solutions and goods. To date the Sainsbury's 'Active Kids' campaign has invested in excess of £185 million into the scheme, trained 9,000 teachers to deliver inclusive activity as part of the 'Active Kids for All' Physical Education training programme and supported over 40,000 schools and youth sports clubs. This example demonstrates the evolution of the action phase of the nexus due to local critiques of ethical and strategic practice of corporations. In this case local populations may only own and gain from what they invest and, therefore, can only experience agency and opportunity through monetary exchange and brand investment.

Educational responses to crisis through sport

Political, social and economic trends often influence educational responses to crisis and global critical issues; in this remit, corporations and business models must follow suit (Ball, 2012; de Lissovoy, 2008;

Evans & Davies, 2015). This has multiple benefits and outcomes for invested stakeholders as trends not only reach public spaces through the media and public debates but also via diverse quasi- and non-governmental, governmental and local agencies. The politically charged and humanitarian refugee crisis is one example of a current critical issue faced by the Global North and a relatively new site for educational development intervention (Banda & Gultresa, 2015; Giulianotti, 2011; Lindsey et al., 2017). Public discourse and social consciousness surrounding this transnational concern have created much traction for the Sport-Education-Corporate nexus, and a response has seen new spaces of local engagement emerge. Of course, local responses have been varied due to the contested nature and social position of refugee populations occupying domestic spaces and this has intersected controversially with the assumed connections of extremism, political violence, poverty and forced connection to 'others'. Despite this, CSR agendas, local activism and national bodies have reacted to the immediate need for social cohesion, integration, psychological and social rehabilitation and economic mobility programmes under the umbrella of sport and education. Toward this pursuit, sport and education have been placed as the universal tools to act and unite.

One such programme has been the Refugee Support Programme (RSP). In collaboration with the UEFA Foundation for Children, the RSP has responded within local contexts throughout Europe. By contextualising the refugee crisis in relation to the significant numbers of children displaced, UEFA have identified a local need. Through the facilitation of *Streetfootballworld* and their corporate partners (Coca-Cola, European Commission, German Foreign Office, FIFA, FedEx and Pro Sky, to name but a few), UEFA has built a curriculum and model of local support based on a complex partnership with governmental and corporate networks. UEFA claim that "In addition to shelter, food and health care, children and youth need educational opportunities, supportive relationships, meaningful social interaction, and opportunities to play with one another so as to ensure their healthy physical and mental development" (https://www.streetfootballworld. org/project/refugee-support-programme-uefa-foundation-children). The RSP provides an opportunity for local 'Football for Good' organisations to apply for funding to enact educational opportunities through football to local refugee and non-refugee populations. The UEFA Foundation for Children currently supports 23 football-based refugee projects across Europe with 1,000,000 EUR in funding. The funding scheme is projected to reach up to 32,000 participants across 15 countries including Belgium, Bosnia and Herzegovina, France,

Georgia, Germany, Greece, Hungary, Ireland, Italy, Serbia, Romania, The Netherlands, the United Kingdom and Ukraine.

Connecting to power contestations, the negotiation of partnerships and transition of local ownership, through the RSP UEFA have advocated and implemented a 'train the train' model of knowledge transference to enable local leaders and educators to prescribe and align the universal and global human rights, educational and social goals. In essence such workshops led by UEFA focus on three primary themes including communication, respect for your fellow players and peaceful conflict resolution. According to UEFA and its partners, these speak to the daily challenges facing refugees and their host communities in this time of transition (ibid.). Arguably this system has both merit and significant flaws. Power in this model is transferred via selection and local implementation has a prescriptive dynamic that systematically controls action. The level at which local populations, both indigenous and those identified as refugees, engaged with these initiatives is debatable, and we might question how social cohesion and education may be achieved if indigenous locals own and implement education to new local groups. The model of funding existing local football for good organisations fuels this important question.

Achieving 'appropriate' action in context

Context in all of these cases matters. Whilst we have aimed to expose connection, symbolic processes, negotiations, competing objectives and power contests across all nexus spaces, at the action stage context is vital. In Jordan, for example, the refugee crisis has exponentially led to a humanitarian, political and social crisis. The UEFA Foundation report that the number of Syrian refugees in Jordan is estimated to be about 1.4 million: 20% live in five camps, and 80% live in urban areas in Northern provinces and around the capital city Amman. Two-thirds of all registered refugees in Jordan are children or teenagers. Lebanon has the highest refugee-to-host population ratio in the world: Over 1.1 million registered refugees for 6.2 million inhabitants. One-third of the total refugee population is 5–18 years old, making this largely a regional crisis affecting children and youth (https://uefafoundation.org/action/empowering-refugee-and-marginalised-children-in-lebanon-and-jordan/). In context, the significant challenges include young people living with uncertainty, psychological effects of trauma, no access to formal education, lack of role models and lack of access to formal and informal learning opportunities for young girls and women (ibid.).

The use of a modified version of the football, Football3, has become the model implemented in Jordan by UEFA and *Streetfootballworld*. Supported by their corporate partners, this model prescribes to a programme of 'three halves'. The three halves include a prematch discussion, a football game and a post-match discussion. The discussion section of the model connects to the key educational themes, such as fair play, gender equality and conflict resolution via dialogue and compromise. This methodology involves local physical and social movement to enact personal and social contact. Lebanese and Jordanian cities/communities act as hosts to facilitate local young populations to engage and integrate, for the prescribed time of the session, with Syrian refugees. In this context time and space again become important to the dynamics of integration, educational opportunities, local control and power over space and physical contact. Congruent with research on refugee programme evaluation (e.g. Doherty & Taylor, 2007; Whitley, Coble & Jewell, 2016), the outcomes and values of such enterprises are difficult to monitor and evaluate as space is not negotiated but opened up for a specific time and purpose; this is closed once the session is complete and the physical movement of refugee and local populations confirm both identity and locally accepted domestic arrangements. Whilst the objective maybe enhanced understanding of the changing ethnic and social landscape at the local level, such programmes may construct diverse perspectives of the local reality and afford oppositional groups to own their indigenous and occupied spaces. As witnessed within the RSP, power here is not negotiated according to the agency and norms of the local context but assumed by dominant locals and their international facilitators to act for education and integration for marginal groups in foreign lands.

Arguably, UEFA and *Streetfootballworld* have recognised the need for diversity in complex contexts. The broadening of the Jordan-Lebanese refugee challenge has been achieved through the support of the German Government, and has equipped local NGOs with football equipment, so they can act in refugee communities in the absence of formal education opportunities. By creating synergies and supporting local NGO structures through training, resources and Football3 events, the time-space continuum may act with enhanced local agency, capacity and consistency. Questionably this is likely to be achieved in the absence of blending diverse populations beyond one-off football3 events. This model is useful for engaging communities and producing discernible actions, yet it also simultaneously exposes the multiple perspectives and everyday realities of local populations and the diverse groups that lie within this social context. Sport, here, is seen as the appropriate tool due to the significant numbers of young refugee populations and its assumed ability to sympathetically incite educational opportunities, unite and encourage personal development after trauma at the local level for both indigenous populations and new inhabitants. Nonetheless, similar to other examples presented in this book, who owns this trend and space is highly contested.

Local innovation through local leaders – who needs corporate backing?

A significant amount of content in this book has focussed on the dependency and norm for local populations and organisations to operate on the premise of corporate funding. This is not contested; corporate capital in most cases is highly sought after and an essential requirement for local organisations to build capacity, develop agency and act upon their knowledge and contextual awareness of their educational needs. However, it is important to also expose the innovations of locals who act in the absence of corporate funding and partnership.

One contemporary example is worth noting here. Throughout 2018, London has seen knife crime rise at an alarming rate, and local news has been consumed by daily reports of stabbings and knife-related killings, largely involving teenagers. Local teenager Jack O'Neill provided national news channels with a story of innovation and action as a response to his personal experience of the knife crime epidemic. Jack coined the phrase 'Knives down, bikes up' and inspired a 3,000 cyclist demonstration through the streets of London to make his case for pursuing cycling over violent crime. Speaking to the BBC Jack remarked, "It really made me think about what I could do to change things in my community... We wanted to bring young people together, take them off the streets and give them something uplifting to do". He thinks riding together makes violence less likely. "They've never been in a fight whilst riding their bikes" (https://www.bbc.co.uk/news/uk-45157728). Through this initiative Jack has founded an organisation that has brought his project to a national audience. Local young people and families can take part in biannual bike rides that bring people and communities together with the intention of showing solidarity toward a critical local issue and demonstrating alternatives to and support for cycling over knife crime and gang violence. In the same BBC report Jack claimed that

> People come and they don't know how to do any tricks. But, they have a great time... As soon as you start slapping rules on kids they aren't interested. So, this allows kids some freedom in a very positive way.

Such personal stories of trauma may form local innovations for education and change and this example exposes the abilities to act in the absence of corporate funding or rigid frameworks of implementation. The power may in some cases rest at the community level from the point of collective thought and reaction to contextual local concerns.

Local sports clubs, such as those exemplified earlier and elsewhere in the sector, are also a source of locally driven action and innovation that may be implemented in the absence of substantial corporate funding. For example, the Grenfell Tower tragedy in London in 2017 saw community action in the aftermath steer and drive local rehabilitation. Although Dale Youth Boxing Club (DYBC) was destroyed in the Grenfell fire, a year later it had been rebuilt and open again to local young people. London Mayor Sadiq Kahn visited the site and claimed,

> What boxing does is give you is life skills: how to be magnanimous in victory, dignified in defeat, and a healthy lifestyle. We've got a problem in obesity and overweight kids – how to keep you fit and active. But also, it gives you a family you can be part of, a sense of belonging. You cheer each other on and let's be frank, you stay out of trouble.
> (https://www.independent.co.uk/sport/general/boxing/grenfell-tower-boxing-dale-youth-club-sadiq-khan-a8563361.html)

Amid the contemporary context and concerns over London's gang and urban violence crisis, the likes of initiatives by DYBC and other similar organisations, who have advocated for boxing and/or sports role in community cohesion and youth development has become increasingly recognised and valued. As the article notes, locally resonant and responsive ventures have shown capacity "in improving countless lives across the capital in the unique way that only sport can" (ibid.). Although local sports clubs may deliver programmes with the assistance of corporate funding and/or economic revenue for local-government-federation sources, many are removed from the nexus due to their embedded place at the local level. With a commitment and often long-standing position within communities, their relationship with local populations is bound by historical heritage, contextual knowledge systems and established insider social position. Boxing provides an appropriate example here, often known for sport's open-door policies, the ability to engage with 'risky' and vulnerable groups, and the sport itself being associated with key educational and soft skills. Corporate and/or State funding maybe desirable, yet in some cases it may not necessarily be essential. As in the case of DYBC, there remains opportunities for locals to act and make meaningful changes in the spaces in which they occupy, understand and are empowered to create educational opportunities aligned to their shared everyday realities.

Conclusion

Corporate presence may not yield in sport education; however, there is a need to preserve, protect, nourish and nurture alternatives that present different ways on thinking, producing and acting, and that keep at the core values that transcend corporate influence. Here we are arguing for a greater recognition among communities and within spaces that there are possibilities to transcend the current power hegemonies that have come to dominate the sport education sector. Moreover, and to embrace the tenets of critical pedagogues, there is potential for challenges to the status quo, for example, in the development of practices that communities decide are meaningful for themselves, that they can take ownership over the means of production and can drive and sustain action on their own terms. As this chapter argue, it is at the action phase of the Sport-Education-Corporate nexus in which there may be a possible return to power for local organisations and populations. As we have witnessed across the vignettes in this and other chapters, a dependency does exist whereby corporations need local groups, expertise and knowledge to provide access to act and implement projects.

Arguably global businesses and those at the top levels of decision-making and influence may have limited understanding or point of reference of the contextual challenges presented and experienced by local communities and organisations. Such complexities are often overlooked with the assumption of locals being passive recipients of development or living without agency. As articulated in these examples, and in our broader investigations and experiences in the sport industry, in many instances local leaders challenge this assumption and through the action stage steer and reshape curriculums to best suit their community needs, such micro-levels of resistance may occur constantly as the local-turn is empowered to eke out this symbiosis in ways that benefit their communities. Communities and local populations must essentially play the game that the corporate stakeholder has designed the terms and conditions for. Such terms and conditions may differ from the original thought; therefore the communities may need to craft particular outcomes to satisfy corporate needs embedded in any partnership. The tension exists when the core principles embedded in sport education initiatives – for example social justice, ethics of care and civic responsibility – are unable to be deployed in the absence of economic imperatives. The local-turn and recognition of local cultural systems and knowledge may see such programmes and processes returning to the humanitarian notions of welfare that are at the heart of community.

This raises important questions with regard to the monitoring and evaluation of sport education programmes. The reporting mechanisms explained throughout this chapter lean toward tokenism, image-based capturing of activity and storytelling. Power in this regard is managed by the locals as communities must respond to the remits of the stakeholder whilst exploring the freedom of exercising their context specific knowledge and cultural adaption to original thoughts of programming and objectives. Much debate has centred on the unheard stories, privileged voices and subjugated knowledge often directing the monitoring and evaluation of sport educational programmes (Nicholls, Giles & Sethna, 2011). The need, and at times absence, of understanding and learning from local populations questions the representation and representativeness at the local level in the first, middle and last instance. There is a clear manipulation and shift of power from the local in this regard, which arguably defines the final stages of the action phase and exposes the fragility of power. The majority of current arrangements are predicated on organisations' exploiting particular communities and spaces wherein there are specific socio-inequalities and disadvantages. The current power arrangement and imbalance works effectively because there is aforementioned dependency. This dependency gives the organisations legitimacy and power; however, if the inequality were removed, so too would be the power imbalance. The cycle of dependency is arguably designed to be sustained.

7 Toward a nexus typology and beyond

Introduction

The vignettes offered in this book provide some illustration that landscapes of sport education are diverse, multilayered, contestable and constantly in flux. This said, in recent decades, there is also a continuity among stakeholders who have retained strategic sector presence. Stakeholders such as FIFA, the IOC, Nike McDonalds and the UN have forged relationships, networks and activities that have consolidated and fortified their roles as sector protagonists, and set the benchmarks, agendas and the tone of future work. These well-known organisations are joined by a raft of other players: For example, charitable and philanthropic foundations, non-governmental agencies, private investors, State departments, international aid and development businesses, and supra/sub-regional and local enterprises. All of whom, variously, aim to utilise sport education to 'facilitate', 'enhance', 'empower', 'inspire' or 'create' change in (most often, young) peoples' lives and communities. As explored in this book and elsewhere, prevailing sport education discourses and developments around the world also speak to capitalising on existing stakeholder activities; encouraging public- and private-sector partnerships; sharing existing geopolitical and/or sociocultural terrain; and developing collaborations for resource acquisition and distribution that better address 'local concerns' and 'communities in need', and result in 'meaningful outcomes and change' (Adams, 2011; Banda & Gultresa, 2015; Burnett, 2014; Coakley, 2011; Gore, 2013; Sanders, Phillips & Vanreusel 2014; Schulenkorf, 2012; Schulenkorf & Edwards, 2012). As such, the continuation and proliferation of corporate interventions and directions within sport education can be viewed in relatively positive ways.

The Sport-Education-Corporate nexus has been a site of advantageous connectivity as stakeholders have been brought together to identify and address enduring and contemporary issues. The nexus, however, is a political and politicised space. Subsequently, developing resolutions to global, regional and/or local ills has also produced contestation as stakeholders negotiate agendas, obligations, responsibilities and accountabilities, and mediate and mitigate involvements in the domestic domain. Yet the nexus affords opportunities for creativity as stakeholder relations, imperatives and knowledge ownership may be reappropriated, resisted or adjusted. To understand these processes, we focussed on how stakeholder connections manifest across spaces of thought, production and action. Such a focus enabled us to appreciate and critique how connections evolve, relationship dynamics are forged and initiatives move from the ideological to the practical.

In this final chapter we consider how our critique might aid further examination of the sport education sector and wider sport industry. Amalgamating examples within the book, we present a preliminary typology (see *Table 7.1*) of the Sport-Education-Corporate nexus that highlights basic synergies and disjuncture in stakeholder intersections, connection characteristics, production themes and action opportunities. We then discuss how issues of sustainability, accountability and ethical representation may need to be furthered. Finally, we consider how these sentiments might transpire on a new collective commons (that evokes the transformative potentialities of Lefebvre's third space) and remain central to responses of those who work in the sector.

The Sport-Education-Corporate typology

When examined individually, examples within this book explain who some primary stakeholders are, the values and agendas they hold, the types of spaces they occupy, why they see sport education as means to corporate ends and what consequences may accrue from their actions. Yet juxtaposed and taken collectively, however, it is possible to develop a more nuanced perspective of the nexus' breadth and reach. Moreover, while for logical and structural reasons we adopted a multi-level analysis (e.g. dividing our critique into rough geographic/geopolitical territories of interest), this formulaic approach has limited our ability to conceptualise the unifiable dimensions of the nexus as an entity. In also following our spatial theoretical orientations (specifically, the heuristic elements of *thought*, *production* and *action*), our investigations presented nexus processes and arrangements in a generally linear way (we respect, as part of this, we strongly emphasised cause-and-e/affect aspects of stakeholder relations). Such an analytical plan enabled us to explain how specific organisations' corporatisation of sport education occurred across time and space, and the myriad ways corporate entities carry out their work from rhetoric to reality. However, by agglomerating the wide range of examples within the book into a nascent typology new features of the nexus begin to emerge, and further points of overlap, tension, disconnection and possibility may also be seen.

Accordingly, in Table 7.1 we present the Sport-Education-Corporate typology. Extending our sector critique, the typology exists as an initial framework to map and examine orientations and behaviours. As an empirical tool, the typology also offers a means to see where new opportunities (or issues and threats) may arise within stakeholder connections and existing hegemonies may be disrupted. Linking to examples covered within this book, the typology comprises four key components: (1) Intersections, (2) Initiative Characteristics, (3) Sociocultural Themes and (4) Opportunities for knowledge ownership. We discuss each of these now, in turn.

Intersections

Congruent with the extant sport sector scholarship, and the context of the nexus, we conceptualise intersections as the points at which individual stakeholders' respective ideas, values, agendas and work join and are forged into (or with) a unified/unifiable imperative or enterprise. For sport, education and corporate stakeholders examined in this research, it is evident that there has been a privileging of certain intersections within the nexus. Four primary intersection types have emerged. The first has been intersections of policy advocacy and implementation. Here stakeholders (e.g. Nike, the Gates Foundation or the IOC) established relationships with partners based on a shared understanding of, and commitment to, the creation of international, regional or national policies. While the precise avenue of policy advocacy and development vary (e.g. the foci may be education, physical education, physical activity, sport or health/well-being), the general intentions remain consolidating multisectoral intervention and/or response to some real (or perceived) globally relevant (yet domestically recognised) epidemiological, public health or social concern. The intersection here is of interest because while corporate entities have the capacity and resource to enact substantive sector change, their influence is afforded further public legitimacy, authenticity and political gravitas when it can be (re)orientated (and reimagined) within recognised structures and processes of policymaking.

Table 7.1 Toward a typology of the Sport-Education-Corporate nexus

Stakeholder	Sport education intersections	Initiative characteristics	Examples	Social/Cultural themes	Opportunities for local knowledge ownership in thought, production and action
Nike (Chapter 4)	• Global and regional policy advocacy, creation • International lead in sport and physical activity network and campaign development • Infrastructure, economic and resource support at local school and community levels	• Development and standardisation of global health, sport, physical activity and lifestyle guidelines • Creation of sector standards and strategies that link explicitly to national and international policy development • Promotion of school-private-sector partnership to facilitate and mobilise global health imperatives	• Let's Move it; Move it: Action for Sport • Designed to Move • 'If I had 5 extra year…' • Community Impact programme	• General health and well-being, aka 'healthy lifestyle' • Youth sport and physical activity promotion • Global obesity and inactivity 'crises' • Broader support for alternative forms of leisure and recreation • Equality of opportunity and experience	• Restricted opportunities to participate in thought and production spaces • Individuals, schools and communities able to engage with directives on their own terms • Individual engagement with health and physical activity promotion
McDonalds (Chapter 4)	• Multifaceted engagements with school curricula	• Emphasis on the development of individuals' social, professional and civic skills	• Community football partnerships and Let's Play	• Healthy lifestyle promotion	• Limited possibilities within the thought space

	• Close collaboration with related sport organisational stakeholders and their associated educational development activity • Infrastructure, economic and resource support at local school and community levels	• Personal and social development through sport and physical education participation • Generation of supportive partnerships to empower local community groups into actions that align with contextually specific health and physical activity ideas	• *Passport to Play* • *My InspirAsian* project • *McTeacher* nights scheme	• Mass sport and physical activity engagement • Individual personal skill development and community socialisation • Incorporation of localised sociocultural content and sport/physical activity specialisation • Ethos of play, enjoyment, fun	• Opportunities for curriculum developers and schools to appropriate knowledge in production • Individual agency exhibited in engagement within local activities
Coca-Cola (Chapter 4)	• Direct involvement in the development and support of formal educational curricula • Sustained support for international-local scale sport education and wider social development work • Economic support for existing sport education ventures in targeted regional and local spaces	• Focus on social mobility via individual and community skill and resource development • Emphasis on community spirit and engagement with sport-related activities • Close reliance on existing stakeholders operating at the regional and local level • Utilises sport and physical activity to leverage the development of individual's business skills	• *Active living* • Coca-Cola foundation scientific and physical activity and education outreach • Alliance with educational organisations, e.g. Cimientos	• Active living as a mechanism of healthy lifestyles • Physical activity promotion through organised sporting activity • Emphasis on social and emotive qualities associated with sport and physical activity • Universal humanity and community connectivity • Utility and accessibility of urban/community space	• In places, clear co-construction of knowledge with schools at the thought and production stage • Contextual knowledge crafting utilising existing connections with educational stakeholders • New knowledge formation possibilities using local urban space

(Continued)

Stakeholder	Sport education intersections	Initiative characteristics	Examples	Social/Cultural themes	Opportunities for local knowledge ownership in thought, production and action
FIFA (Chapter 5)	• Sport-specific leader in the football related educational and social development • Utilisation of national and supra-regional networks and existing sport structure and school connections, to aid education outreach • Targeted educational and developmental projects	• Focus on personal/interpersonal and professional skill development via sport participation • Synergise with school and community sport and physical activity agendas • Promotion of civic ideals deemed appropriate to communities 'in need' • Close associations between professional sport performance and mass participation agendas	• Football for hope • Football for peace	• Provision of global aid • Sport for peace agendas • Humanitarianism and promotion of universal civic values • Eradication of socio-economic inequalities	• Contextual knowledge construction occasionally occurs with individuals and community leaders • Close dependency on extant educational organisations to facilitate communication and programme translation • Potential for local reappropriation once corporate organisation retreats
IOC (Chapter 5)	• Global lead in sport education and sport-related social development activities	• Strong emphasis on the development of universal moral pedagogies via sport participation	• Olympic Values Education Programme (OVEP)	• Universal humanity and community connectivity	• Limited participation of local stakeholders at the thought and production stages (with the exception of some National Olympic Committees and countries)

	• Sustained development and control over formal education projects related to the Olympic movement • Promote, support and lobby for the dissemination of education interventions at the regional and local levels	• Promotion of core values aligned to the principles and ethos of the organisation • Strategic and direct intervention in formal curriculum development • Creation of education resources to augment and supplant regional and local activities • Close associations between professional sport performance and mass participation agendas	• *International global active city* • *Getset* – (digital Olympic education platform)	• Provision of global aid • Sport for peace agendas • Eradication of socio-economic inequalities • Morality, ethics and values-based pedagogies • Championing of civil liberties and political freedoms via sport	• Some opportunities for knowledge contextualisation within specified programme activities • Level of engagements and autonomy may still reside with practitioners
Philanthropic Foundations (Chapter 5)	• Wide scale education, social and educational outreach that on occasion may intersect with/involve sport • Resource and economic support for community sport and physical activity initiatives	• Less emphasis of development of education material • Sport and physical activity resources developed to align with broader regional and local projects	• *50million strong* campaign • *SHAPE* network	• Servitude toward the disempowered, socio-economically disadvantaged and under-resourced • Civic/community duty aka 'giving back'	• Frequent engagement with local communities, groups and individuals in the thought and production spaces • Reliance on local educational providers to facilitate the translation of production outcomes

(Continued)

Stakeholder	Sport education intersections	Initiative characteristics	Examples	Social/Cultural themes	Opportunities for local knowledge ownership in thought, production and action
	• Indirect formal curricula involvement, support related to broader sport/physical activity engagements and opportunities • Regional and local level sport commitments often specifically designed to augment existing corporate focus	• Development of education training programmes that promote health and well-being to disadvantaged and under-resourced groups • Sport/Physical activity promotion used as a mechanism of addressing social and economic inequality	• *Beyond sport* project • Contributions to sport relief • *Kids on course* • Partnerships with non-governmental organisations, e.g. Right to play	• Public health, well-being and lifestyle promotion • Large scale network collaboration	• Some opportunities to take ownership of knowledge, yet this may be constrained by reliance on funding and resources • Local individual and communities may shift position and agendas to capitalise on sector/stakeholder priorities
Local community-orientated organisations	• Direct engagement with local communities agencies and individuals	• Development of a bespoke sport (e.g.≈boxing/football) programme	• *Streetworldfootball*	• Equality of opportunity	• Programmes designed to be dynamic and contextually resonant and responsive

• Collaborations forged around achieving unity and conflict/tension resolution • Provision of sport-related humanitarian aid • Alleviating socio-economic disadvantage and the politics of inequality	• Promotion of cross-cultural/community dialogue • Ethnic and/or cultural exchange • Promotion of international relations and community solidarity	• *Refugee support programme* • *Dale youth boxing club*	• Local and/or global harmony and cohesion • Youth and civic development • Personal and collective skill development • Sensitivities and sensibilities demonstrated toward ethnic, cultural, religious and economic divisions and inequalities	• At the outset, requires buy-in from local spaces • Opportunities for engagement and participations that reflect individuals' and communities' *in situ* concerns • Local constituents afforded ownership and voice in the conceptualisation, development, implementation and evaluation

The second aspect of intersectionality involves connections related to social/community responsibility. This aspect may be unsurprising, given the emphasis that organisations within and beyond sport have placed on Corporate Social Responsibility (CSR) in recent decades and that CSR comprises direct connections between corporations and external entities. Nonetheless, demonstrating commitments to social and community spaces is, evidently, fundamental to connections across the nexus. That connections are established on this point also makes sense considering the pervasive assumptions about sports' humanitarian/humanistic qualities and the inherent beliefs in sport educations' transformative capacities. This said, such is the entrenched nature of social and community development in the sector that it may be argued that it has become a defining, and inescapable, raison d'être for sector relations. This is especially so if those relations are to be viewed positively and productively within the capitalistic environments and operations to which they are a part. In themselves, intersections formed as part of CSR are not necessarily problematic. However, as has been discussed throughout this book, CSR is a value-laden and political act that, despite having communities' 'best' interests at heart, may not start from a point of mutual understanding, comprises equitable participation and ownership, recognises or respects the sensitivities of stakeholders, or leads to sustainable or meaningful outcomes. Irrespective of these issues, an ethos of responsibility can be clearly recognised as part of the Sport-Education-Corporate nexus.

The third identifiable element of intersection is curriculum development (namely, within the discipline of Physical education but also extending into other subjects and domains, including health and personal welfare, social studies/development and citizenship). Here, there has been a twofold approach. The first involves sport and corporate entities (e.g. FIFA, Coca-Cola and National Olympic Committees) explicitly positioning themselves as educational providers, a feat achieved by developing teaching and learning materials that directly align to global education concepts (e.g. Fair play, citizenship, international awareness) and provide pedagogical content and links to domestic educational curricula. Intersections here are fortified by strategic collaborations with policy-makers, curricula developers, individual schools/school networks and related education or sport-based service providers. Second, there are intersections involving indirect stakeholder participation in curriculum development. Such an approach may be seen in regional and local spaces (such as those examined in Chapters 5 and 6) whereby corporate stakeholders work in concert with schools and existing educational-support providers to augment, supplement or provide contrasting alternatives to existing curricula. This approach is apparent in the work of McDonalds, Nike, the Aegon TransAmerica Foundation and the Gates Foundation, where educational collaborations build off existing curricula frameworks and provide resources to augment programme content.

The forth aspect relates to connections enhancing infrastructure and resource provision. Across the nexus, most stakeholder collaborations were framed, to varying degrees, by a commitment to support resourcing and infrastructure change (e.g. providing financial support for equipment, personnel, training or built environments or establishing management structures or networks to continue the delivery and monitoring of specific programmes). Reflecting the economically and politically favourable position large corporate entities are frequently in, offering resource and infrastructure assistance as a platform for stakeholder connection is logical. Nonetheless, as outlined in Chapter 2, as altruistic as such offers may seem, they also reflect that in corporate terms relationships between partners are often premised on inequalities that create unfavourable power imbalances and adversely affect the equity of bargaining process (in terms of the nexus, we rehearse here the difficulty of socio-economically deprived communities to resist corporate assistance).

We are not implying there that communities (or more often individuals within communities) have no power and capacity to negotiate, or mitigate the effects of, resource offers and infrastructure changes (a point well highlighted in Chapter 6). Rather, our contention here is that in many cases nexus intersections *rely* on the need to provide resources and infrastructure support. Without this remit, there is the possibility that some points of intersection would lose substance and meaning (or organisations may be required to consider other ways of connecting). Also, what emerges here is that while there may always be individuals, communities and spaces in need, *if* corporate stakeholders are successful in their missions to resource and provide infrastructure in some spaces it might then be possible to question the necessities of their CSR practices in that locale. Consider, for instance, what might transpire if the Football Association in the United Kingdom succeeded in equipping all grass-roots clubs and schools with the facilities, personnel and funds to ensure that all young people who wanted to play football could do so, and/or local communities became self-sustaining. What if, furthermore, local communities became self-sustaining, and their reliance on the Football Association's CSR diminished? Such a vision may appear idealistic, but we raise it here to illustrate that while intersections can be forged for different reasons, and appear strong and indelible, they are premised on assumptions that are at times fragile and can (and should) be challenged. In this case, such assumptions include beliefs about what sport and education are, who it should be for, what sport education spaces 'look' like, what constitutes 'a need'/'disadvantage'/'issue' and who should benefit from intervention and how. It is useful to note here, too, that intersection types are not mutually exclusive but, rather, overlap and are intertwined. In addition, these points of intersections may be more latent than explicit.

Initiative characteristics

While there is apparent commonality in nexus stakeholders' intersections, there are further synergies in the characteristics of collaboration initiatives. We refer here essentially to what the general focus of intersectional thought is and what the specific initiative idea comprises. Again, reflecting the humanitarian ethos that pervades throughout the nexus, most intersections can be characterised as serving an altruistic imperative: Namely to improve social harmony, community relations or citizenship. As part of this mission, sport/physical activity participation becomes *the* mechanism of social change. To this end, one characteristic stakeholder initiatives share is in how they frame their respective work within the context of addressing global health and physical activity imperatives. Key in this regard is in the utility of sport education to drive social mobility, civic responsibility and the development of core personal and professional skills (that, in turn and time, might collectively contribute to resolving global and local public health crises).

Stakeholders vary slightly in what their initiative foci are. Nike, UNESCO and the IOC, for instance, focus on establishing international networks and alliances that create global health and physical activity benchmarks. McDonalds and FIFA, in comparison, develop close local school synergies that harness community spirit. Nonetheless, the underlying characteristics are largely comparable and predictable. Initiatives frequently start from a point of recognising, concomitantly, that (1) some form of universal participatory and/or inactivity crises exists, and (2) there is an unquestionable collective desire to celebrate humanity through physicality and health behaviour. Subsequently, there is typically a connection between the global ailments, the proposed organisational panacea (namely, some specific form of sport education CSR relief), and the benefits to, and responsibilities of, specific communities and/or individuals. What follows, depending on the space or temporal contexts, is frequently the use of either sport-mega-event (e.g. the Olympic or Commonwealth Games or World Cups) or professional or elite sporting competitions or athletes (e.g. Premier League football competition or use of renowned athletes), or national/domestic sport trends to provide a popular cultural reference and resonance that may inspire engagement (frequently measured in terms of mass participation). As seen in the IOC and the London Organising Committee for the Olympic Games' Olympic education initiatives, FIFA's *Football for Hope* Campaign or Nike's *Designed to Move* campaign, the rhetoric is framed in such a way that communities/individuals are directly complicit in both humanities' problems and its solutions. The moral undertones here matter in that they afford the protagonist corporations a 'hook' by which to captivate (and capture) necessary audiences, an ethical cause with which to identify and an emotional connection that may compel communities/individual to take the desired action (irrespective of previous interests in either sport/physical activity or the corporate entities involved).

Themes

As varied as collaborative initiatives are, within action spaces prevalent themes have emerged. In essence, initiative themes are unsurprising and largely reflect pervasive discourses across (and beyond) the sport sector that: (a) There are universal concerns to be addressed; (b) collaborative ventures are not only warranted but necessary; (c) addressing concerns necessitates substantive consensus regarding priorities, objectives and outcomes; and (d) within the sector, top-down global sport organisation synergies are the most preferred mechanism of delivery. While there are evident caveats regarding these discourses (e.g. that countervailing positions are also at play), by-in-large they can be easily identified within the nexus. Across the examples we examined, several universal themes are evident. Notably these are epidemiological commitments to enhance healthy and physical activity behaviour (frequently, obesity crises and/or inactivity prevention), building capacity for peace and community development, the eradication of inequality and the proselytising of universal civic and moral values. As far as available empirical evidence suggests, these themes reflect discernible and laudable humanitarian concerns worthy of collective and individual investment. Moreover, such themes provide clear, specific and potentially meaningful points for establishing stakeholder connections. In addition, at a time when structural and economic forces have orientated organisational governance agendas toward greater performativity, identifiable impacts, ensuring sustainability and social investment, contributions to these global agendas makes strategic sense and enable nexus stakeholders to effectively 'do their bit for the *a/the* cause'.

These themes may be representative of nexus connections, yet they also belie other ideas and concerns that emerge in collaborative spaces. These may include, for instance: Diversity and inclusion (as already evident in some of the sport education initiatives that adopt multiculturalism or individual pluralism or sport development initiatives that adopt grass-roots advocacy and cultural cognisant praxis) (see also Hayhurst, 2011; Thorpe, Hayhurst & Chawansky, 2018), critical responses to existing economic and political structures (e.g. initiatives challenging the burdens sport-corporate relations place on communities related to 'legacy') and localised responses of anti-sport/anti-globalisation/corporatisation activism that might destabilise the nexus' hold on particular domestic terrain. Such themes matter because they address a recognised need to decolonise sport spaces, that is, challenge organisation practices that have replaced indigenous knowledges, identity constructions and representations. Although stakeholders within the nexus may not, inherently, desire to supplant local values and belief systems, by virtue of extensively proselytising a rhetoric of universalism (e.g. philosophies of Olympism, 'sport-for-all' calls, privileging of dominant (namely, Western) sport tropes and practices), there is a degree of ideological sanitisation occurring that may inhibit alternate modes of meaning making. Tentative as the typology may be, and while themes, characteristics and relations may be generalised, what they begin to identify is a prioritising of actions, initiatives and agendas within the nexus related to prevailing assumptions about global needs, concerns and desires. Furthermore, it is difficult to ignore that these decisions comprise a set of power relations (in this case, between key global sport and corporate and education stakeholders, predominately of the well-resourced Global North) that have been instrumental in crystallising the status quo vis-à-vis sport/physical activity and sport education as commodifiable entities of public health, international diplomacy and community development.

Opportunities

There are several opportunities within the nexus whereby knowledge ownership (as conceptualised by *who* produces, *what* is produced and *how* it is shared) is, or might be, devolved, shared or shifted. The first possibilities arise from stakeholders' respective efforts to create universally applicable responses to global ills. While acknowledging the issues of the universalism entrenched within nexus actions, the wide-scope of most programmes ultimately means that individuals have a degree of agency in deciding whether to engage and/or appropriately aspects of the programmes are most meaningful within their lives and contexts. Although such agency may be more perceptual than practical (e.g. in the case of formal Olympic education programmes that are mandated within curricula and rolled-out in classes irrespective of young peoples' needs or sporting interests), there may still be space to mediate the terms of corporate engagement or extent of buy-in to prevailing regimes of thought.

The point here regarding individual potentialities within the nexus is a seminal one that, we recognise, deserves investigation outside the scope of our existing work. However, we have witnessed times and spaces in this and other research in which decisions to engage or not engage with sport education programmes and corporate activity have strongly resided at the level of the individual or community. Freedom of choice, for example, exists occasionally in how programmes may be delivered, promoted and engaged with (as discussed in the previous chapter with regard to local spaces). While some programmes may be delivered according to institutional imperatives, logic and ideology (such is the case often with FIFA or IOC actions), practitioners charged with delivery may still have opportunities to contextualise content, change delivery mechanisms or potential audiences and alter the emphasis on certain ideals and values. Similarly, positive approaches to knowledge co-creation are also undertaken in other corners of the nexus. In some countries – for example New Zealand, the United Kingdom and Japan – local schools have contributed to the production of corporate-led regionally or locally specific sport/physical education initiatives (e.g. as evident in the efforts of some National Olympic Committees and/or Local Olympic Games Organising Committees (OGOC), for example, the Tokyo 2020 OGOC). In addition, open-source platforms have emerged that democratise content and remove practical, legal and economic barriers to resource access and use (e.g. as seen in the *Kent20in12* programme). Elsewhere, partnerships have been fostered that incorporate local decisionmakers within the sport education initiative construction (to note, aspects of philanthropic foundation programmes often do this, though largely to ensure community buy-in; moreover, local representation is often a political strategy toward resource acquisition). Such examples are by no means definitive or exhaustive, and we respect that the success of reconfiguring knowledge ownership within the Sport-Education-Corporate nexus comes with significant caveats. Least of all that any emancipatory or empowerment efforts still reside within a neo-liberal market context. Notwithstanding conditions and context, we remain optimistic about where creative seeds of action may currently exist or may yet exist in the future. To this end, the generation of a typology is useful in demonstrating that, while nexus activities may vary, there are congruities among stakeholders that may warrant further investment. In addition, as a preliminary mapping exercise, the typology is of value in exhibiting nexus relations, where contestation and challenges reside, and where connections inhibit or nurture new sites of progressive thought, production and action.

Sustaining nexus relations to forge a creative, critical and caring commons

At present, we are at an evident juncture at which several dominant sport and non-sport-corporate entities hold substantial power over the development of sport, physical activity/education, health and well-being discourses, imperatives and activities. Prevailing global political and economic forces have provided an amiable environment for industry collaboration and legitimised stakeholder connectivity and power relations, and have created a landscape in which sport, education and corporate alliances are normalised and fortified. The nexus, however, does not represent an impasse for reconfiguring ways we think and do in sport, and or present insurmountable barriers to how sport might better serve individuals' and communities' needs. As evidenced throughout this book and elsewhere, the concern is not that sport education has become a site of corporate occupation per se or that this is inherently problematic. Indeed, we recognise, and see witnessed across global, regional and local spaces, that sports' educational value, coupled with the popularity of sport/physical activity and moral connections between physicality and global epidemiology, has made it an attractive commodity and a dynamic commercial space, a direct consequence of which has been large-scale investment into infrastructure, resources and initiatives that have positively affected people's lives and collective experiences. In this crude sense, money does matter, and it would be naïve to think that degrees of commodification and commercialisation do not have a place in the production of contemporary sport education acts. Moreover, as much as stakeholder connections may depend on the intangible qualities of goodwill, trust, a sharing of obligations and burdens, and mutual respect and shared understanding, most relations (at least in the examples we examined) comprise important economic agreements and financial expectations that form integral parts of the legal and political partnerships. There are, of course, times in which the economic 'cost' of stakeholder investment may be offset or become less of a priority: For example, when stakeholders undertake philanthropic enterprise. Nonetheless, there are still economic processes at work here that underpin the collaborations and, in the many cases where there are resource inequities between partners, may beget issues of dependency, exploitation and expectation. This may be the current state of play, yet the point here is that while spaces of thought, production and action may have been colonised, that colonisation is neither total nor final. Furthermore, while it may be relatively easy to vilify the presence and effects of corporatisation within the sport education sector, it is as necessary to recognise that there are (however at times latent) ethical dimensions to the nexus that deserve consideration.

Given how extensive the array of current corporate-driven sport education provision is, the vast number of individuals, groups and communities who have been afforded sport participation opportunities, and the range of initiatives produced to respond to global concerns, it is difficult to deny that stakeholders' efforts are without an ethical dimension. Or, at the very least, an element of care among stakeholders for what they do, how they do it or who they do it to/ with. The organisations illustrated in our examination appear, at least invariably, to exhibit degrees of ethical concern when they transpose themselves onto individuals' lives and community spaces and engage with global, regional and/or local priorities. Here then, it is useful to return briefly to broader understandings of care to appreciate a critique of nexus relations might be approached by resurrecting fundamental ethical aspects already residing within sport spaces (and/or that might be encouraged in the first instance at the point of human(e) connectivity). As various scholars suggest (e.g. Held, 2006; Oruc & Sarikaya, 2011; Tronto, 1993), an ethics of care, however, can be difficult to identify and, as a holistic construct, naturally defies the sorts of measurement, evaluation and monitoring practices that the sector has come to demand of sport organisation relations within the nexus. Yet notions of care have not readily been examined within stakeholder relations in the sport sector. Furthermore, considerations of care have been supplanted by, and consumed synonymously within, the predominant focus on CSR.

Although social responsibility has become a defining characteristic of sector relations, its use and the subsequent critique (Held, 2006; Koggel & Orme, 2010; McEwan & Goodman, 2010; Tronto, 1993) have masked and limited the ways in which ethical practices generally, and care specifically, may be manifest. The conflation of care with social responsibility, and the overemphasis on the latter, has essentially reduced stakeholders' demonstrations of care to a series of derivative, visible (aka public) and quantifiable (thus measurable) criteria that have become closely tied to organisational performativity, community engagement objectives and 'good' governance imperatives. Such is this enmeshment within the nexus that to not attend to social responsibility may be considered not only 'bad' business/'bad' for business but also tantamount to condemnable ethical decisions *not* to care. The issue is that, in effect, care has been reduced from its broadest conceptualisation and application (one in which, Tronto (1993), McEwan and Goodman (2010), and Oruc and Sarikaya (2011) contend, entails empathy, compassion, justice and love, cultural sensitivity and sensibility, value-free understanding, transparency) to an outcome orientation. Such a construction is, we note, clearly evidenced in spaces where stakeholders link their capacity to care to the provision of financial aid and resources. Care in the nexus, essentially, has become an economic rather than ethical transaction. This is not, however, to say that organisations do not demonstrate a genuine intention *to* care but rather that the meaningfulness of this care is mitigated by the economic conditions and corporate context of obligation in which the exchange takes place.

Our call, thus, is for a dialogue about care ethics to be (or remain if it exists already) fundamental and foremost in stakeholder relations. Such a position aligns with guiding pedagogues' encouragements for sustained educational advocacy underscored by ethical ontologies of empowerment and justice, and echo Lefebvre's (1991a, 1991b; Shields, 1999) thesis regarding the necessity of a third space, a site of critical reorientation that redresses hegemonic practice and provides new ways thinking, knowing and doing. Stakeholders may approach this call in varied ways, yet fresh direction may be forged, in the first instance, by adopting a reflexive mode of enquiry. Reflexivity might question, variously: Whether stakeholders within the nexus can moderate corporate imperatives and charitable endeavours beyond that which can be/ needs to be measured in economic terms; whether drives to increase the scope and capacity of existing programmes (which many examples in this book claim to aspire to) are appropriate; whether corporate intervention in certain spaces is actually necessary; whether social responsibility should be foremost community driven; and if, at the most practical level, resources, infrastructure and support can be more freely given without expectation and obligation (e.g. in terms of delivering to set corporate agendas and enabling localised decision-making).

As intimated previously, such introspection is occurring in corners of the nexus. Yet further work remains, not just for corporate stakeholders but also for individuals and communities in local spaces, who also have roles to play in this reconfiguration. To this end, new relations may be established by questioning how individuals, schools, communities and groups enhance their political agency and can be better resourced to mediate or resist corporate interventionism, or at least have a stronger voice in how nexus stakeholders engage in local spaces. Part of this may require a rethink of the wider sustainability of nexus and for local constituents to more frequently interrogate what they might want and need out of their relationships.

Conclusion

We began this book by recognising the distinct interplay sport, education and corporate entities are engaged with and the consequences this intersectionality has on some of the political, economic and socio-cultural characteristics of global, regional and local spaces. To understand the complexities of connections within and across sector spaces we proposed the idea of the Sport-Education-Corporate nexus, essentially as a recognition of a fertile collective commons in which sport has an acknowledged pedagogical potential that has been arrested and recrafted with commercial contours. Such a packaging of sport, and its strategic (re)positioning within wider universal public health, physical activity and well-being and civic agendas make understanding the underlying ideological and structural mechanisms of the sector of interest and value. To this end, and while recognising non-linear, fragmented and unknowable aspects of sector activity, we focussed on how some stakeholders interact in thought, production and action spaces. While stakeholder collaborations, orientations and initiatives vary, our assessment revealed evident patterns of assumptions, behaviours and actions that characterise the sector and that have come to constitute a strong consolidation of power (which we codified, to an extent, in the previous typology). Such positionality is not immutable but rather may be destabilised and held to account by forms of spatial activism, resistance and negotiation.

Respecting the limitations of our work, we end by proposing a few research lines that might form part of a continued collective inquisition of the nexus. In the first instance, and reflecting our own backgrounds, we see opportunities for further utilisation of multi-sector, interdisciplinary and theoretically grounded works that might provide novel interrogations of the breadth and depth of sector partnerships.

Part of this activity might also entail critique of sector partnerships and activities (beyond those of the well-known organisations). Noting the dearth of available scholarship there is a desperate need for more substantive examination of philanthropic foundations' relations within sport. While work has considered the varied roles of sport and non-sport-specific community charities, larger entities that do not exclusively focus on sport have avoided detailed scrutiny. Future work may yet examine more elements and connections between thought, production and action spaces, and (encouraged by the likes of Lefebvre and Tuan) do so not just in a linear fashion but also in ways that recognise dynamic, cyclical and complex machinations. We also encourage investigations that could articulate a greater array of stakeholder voices and positions (including qualitative and quantitative studies that amalgamate corporate and educational entity decision makers with accounts of service providers, practitioners and recipients) (see also Nishtar, 2004; Walters & Chadwick, 2009). This might entail, we envision, closer scrutiny of the covert ways in which corporate partnerships are shaping global health agendas and informing national policy development and implementation; though with stronger emphasis on holding public-private partnerships to account (e.g. in the manner explored beyond sport by Börzel & Risse, 2005, Kaul, 2006; Piggin, 2015). Lastly, reflecting the progressive ways in which sport organisations and corporate affiliates are orientating their marketing strategies to reflect demographic shifts, there needs to be greater attention toward how digital spaces and/or social media technologies are being utilised as part of nexus consolidation and development. We take inspiration from scholars (e.g. Dees, 2011; Hayhurst, Wilson & Frisby, 2011; Wilson & Hayhurst, 2009) who are already paving this path.

To end, the ideas we espouse here are seeds we believe might inspire, challenge or at least provoke thought and provide encouragement to others working in the field. Continued appraisals of the sporting commons may do well to further some of the ideas within the book, and in doing so, we hope new, critical and creative enterprises may transpire. It is to this task that our collective scholarly efforts should be directed.

References

Adams, A. (2011) 'Between modernisation and mutual aid: The changing perceptions of Voluntary sports clubs in England', *International Journal of Sports Policy and Politics, 3* (1): 23–43.

Aegon Transamerica Foundation (2016) *Annual report.* Atlanta, GA: ATF

Amsler, S. S. (2011) 'From 'therapeutic' to political education: The centrality of affective sensibility in critical pedagogy', *Critical Studies in Education, 52* (1): 47–46.

Anaf, J., Baum, F. E., Fisher, M., Harris, E., & Friel, S. (2017) 'Assessing the health impact of transnational corporations: A case study on McDonald's Australia', *Globalization and Health, 13* (1): 7.

Anagnostopoulos, C., Gillooly, L., Cook, D., Parganas, P., & Chadwick, S. (2017) 'Stakeholder communication in 140 characters or less: A study of community sport foundations', *VOLUNTAS: International Journal of Voluntary and Nonprofit Organizations, 28* (5): 2224–2250.

Anderson, E. D. (2009) 'The maintenance of masculinity among the stakeholders of sport', *Sport Management Review, 12* (1): 3–14.

Andrews, D. (2016) 'Sport, spectacle and the politics of late capitalism', In Bairner, A., Kelly, J., & Woo Lee, J. (eds.) *Routledge handbook of sport and politics.* Oxon: Routledge, pp. 225–237.

Andrews, D. L., & Silk, M. L. (2018) 'Sport and neoliberalism: An affective-ideological articulation', *The Journal of Popular Culture, 51* (2): 511–533.

Aspen Institute (2015) *Sport for all, play for life: A playbook to get every kid in the game.* Aspen, CO: Aspen Institute.

Bakir, A., Blodgett, J. G., & Salazar, R. J. (2017) 'Corporate sponsorships in schools: Altruism and ethical judgments', *Journal of Promotion Management, 23* (1): 80–99.

Bale, J., & Vertinsky, P. (eds.). (2004) *Sites of sport: Space, place, experience.* New York: Routledge.

Ball, S. J. (2012) *Global education Inc.: New policy networks and the neoliberal imaginary.* New York: Routledge.

Banda, D., & Gultresa, I. (2015) 'Using Global South Sport-for-Development experiences to inform Global North CSR design and implementation: A case study of Euroleague Basketball's One Team programme', *Corporate Governance, 15* (2): 196–213.

Banks, H. (2016) 'The business of peace: Coca-Cola's contribution to stability, growth, and optimism', *Business Horizons, 59* (5): 455–461.

Barkan, J. (2011) "Got dough?': How billionaires rule our schools', *Dissent, 58* (1): 49–57. *Project MUSE*, muse.jhu.edu/article/407325.

Bartley, T., & Kincaid, D. (2016) 'The mobility of industries and the limits of corporate social responsibility: Labor codes of conduct in Indonesian factories', *Corporate Responsibility in a Globalizing World*, 393–429, DOI: 10.1017/CBO9781316162354.012

Batts, C., & Andrews, D. L. (2011) "Tactical athletes': The United States Paralympic Military Program and the mobilization of the disabled soldier/athlete', *Sport in Society, 14* (5): 553–568.

Batty, R. J. (2016) 'Understanding stakeholder status and legitimate power exertion within community sport events: A case study of the Christchurch (New Zealand) City to Surf', In Jepson, A. & Clarke, A. (eds.) *Managing and developing communities, festivals and events*. London: Palgrave Macmillan, pp. 103–119.

Bell, K., McNaughton, D., & Salmon, A. (eds.). (2011) *Alcohol, tobacco and obesity: Morality, mortality and the new public health*. London: Routledge.

Black, D. R. (2010) 'The ambiguities of development: Implications for 'development through sport', *Sport in Society, 13* (1): 121–129.

Blum, D., & Ullman, C. (2012) 'The globalization and corporatization of education: The limits and liminality of the market mantra', *International Journal of Qualitative Studies in Education, 25* (4): 367–373.

Boler, M. (2004) 'Teaching for hope: The ethics of shattering world views', In Liston, D. & Garrison, J. (eds.) *Teaching, learning and loving: Reclaiming passion in educational practice*. New York: Routledge, pp. 117–131.

Boler, M., & Zembylas, M. (2003) 'Discomforting truths: The emotional terrain of understanding difference', In Trifonas, P. (ed.) *Pedagogies of difference: Rethinking education for social change*. New York: Routledge, pp. 115–138.

Börzel, T. A., & Risse, T. (2005). Public-private partnerships: Effective and legitimate tools of international governance. In Grande, E. & Pauly, L. W. (eds.) *Complex sovereignty: Reconstructing political authority in the twenty first century*, Toronto: University of Toronto Press, pp. 195–216.

Bourdieu, P. (1978) 'Sport and social class', *Information (International Social Science Council), 17* (6): 819–840.

Bridoux, F., & Stoelhorst, J. W. (2014) 'Microfoundations for stakeholder theory: Managing stakeholders with heterogeneous motives', *Strategic Management Journal, 35* (1): 107–125.

Bryson, J. M. (2004) 'What to do when stakeholders matter: Stakeholder identification and analysis techniques', *Public Management Review, 6* (1): 21–53.

Burbules, N., & Berk, R. (1999) 'Critical thinking and critical pedagogy: Relations, differences and limits', In Popkewitz, T. & Fendler, L. (eds.) *Critical theories in education: Changing terrains of knowledge and politics.* London: Routledge, pp. 45–65.

Burgelman, R. A. (2017) 'Complex strategic integration at Nike: Strategy process and strategy-as-practice', In Floyld, S. W. & Wooldridge, B. (eds.) *Handbook of middle management strategy process research,* Cheltenham: Edward Elgar, pp. 197–242.

Burnett, C. (2014) 'The impact of a sport-for-education programme in the South African context of poverty', *Sport in Society, 17* (6): 722–735.

Burnett, C. (2015) 'Assessing the sociology of sport: On sport for development and peace', *International Review for the Sociology of Sport, 50* (4–5): 385–390.

Carden, L. L., Maldonado, T., & Boyd, R. O. (2018) 'Organizational resilience: A look at McDonald's in the fast food industry', *Organizational Dynamics, 47* (1): 25–31.

Carroll, A., & Buchholtz, A. (2014) *Business and society: Ethics, sustainability, and stakeholder management.* Toronto: Nelson Education.

Carter, M. A., Signal, L., Edwards, R., & Hoek, J. (2018) 'Competing teammates: Food in New Zealand sports settings', *Health Promotion International.* doi:10.1093/heapro/day035.

Castro-Martinez, M. P., & Jackson, P. R. (2015) 'Collaborative value co-creation in community sports trusts at football clubs', *Corporate Governance, 15* (2): 229–242.

Chatziefstathiou, D. (2011) 'Olympism: A learning philosophy for physical education and youth sport', In Armour, K. M. (ed.) *Introduction to sport pedagogy for teachers and coaches: Effective learners in physical education and youth sport.* Harlow: Pearson, p.90–101

Chatziefstathiou, D. (2012a) 'Olympic education and beyond: Olympism and value legacies from the Olympic and Paralympic Games', *Educational Review, 64* (3): 385–400.

Chatziefstathiou, D. (2012b) 'Active citizens and policy: The example of London 2012 Olympic Games', *International Journal of Sport Management, Recreation and Tourism, 9,* 23–33.

Chelladurai, P. (2016) 'Corporate social responsibility and discretionary social initiatives in sport: A position paper', *Journal of Global Sport Management, 1* (1–2): 4–18.

Clarke, T. (2004) 'Cycles of crisis and regulation: The enduring agency and stewardship problems of corporate governance', *Corporate Governance: An International Review, 12* (2): 153–161.

Coakley, J. (2011) 'Youth sports: What counts as "positive development"?' *Journal of Sport and Social Issues, 35* (3): 306–324.

Coalter, F. (2010) 'The politics of sport-for-development: Limited focus programmes and broad gauge problems?' *International Review for the Sociology of Sport, 45* (3): 295–314.

Coalter, F. (2013) *Sport for development: What game are we playing?* New York: Routledge.

Coburn, A., & McCafferty. P. (2016) 'The real Olympic Games: Sponsorship, schools and the Olympics – the case of Coca-Cola', *Taboo: The Journal of Culture and Education, 15* (1): 23–40.

Cody, K., & Jackson, S. (2016) 'The contested terrain of alcohol sponsorship of sport in New Zealand', *International Review for the Sociology of Sport, 51* (4): 375–393.

Collins, T. (2013) *Sport in capitalist society: A short history.* Oxon: Routledge.

Collison, H., Darnell, S., Giulianotti, R., & Howe, P. D. (2017a) 'The inclusion conundrum: A critical account of youth and gender issues within and beyond sport for development and peace interventions', *Social Inclusion, 5* (2): 223–231.

Collison, H., Darnell, S., Giulianotti, R., & Howe, P. D. (2017b) 'Sport for social change and development: Sustaining transnational partnerships and adapting international curriculums to local contexts in Rwanda', *International Journal of the History of Sport, 33* (15): 1685–1699.

Collison, H., Giulianotti, R., Howe, P. D., & Darnell, S. (2016) 'The methodological dance: Critical reflections on conducting a cross-cultural comparative research project on 'Sport for Development and Peace', *Qualitative Research in Sport, Exercise and Health, 8* (5): 413–423.

Corsaro, D., Ramos, C., Henneberg, S. C., & Naudé, P. (2012) 'The impact of network configurations on value constellations in business markets—The case of an innovation network', *Industrial Marketing Management, 41* (1): 54–67.

Cote, M., Day, R., & de Peuter, G. (eds.). (2007) *Utopian pedagogy: Radical experiments against neoliberal globalization.* Toronto: University of Toronto Press.

Culpan, I., & Wigmore, S. (2010) 'The delivery of Olympism Education within a Physical education context drawing on critical pedagogy', *International Journal of Sport and Health Sciences, 8,* 67–76.

Darnell, S. C. (2010) 'Power, politics and "sport for development and peace": Investigating the utility of sport for international development', *Sociology of Sport Journal, 27* (1): 54–75.

Darder, A., Baltodano, M., & Torres, R. D. (eds.). (2003) *The critical pedagogy reader.* New York: Routledge.

Davies, A. (2016) *Best practice in corporate governance: Building reputation and sustainable success.* New York: Routledge.

Davies, B., & Bansel, P. (2007) 'Neoliberalism in education', *International Journal of Qualitative Studies in Education, 20* (3): 247–259.

Davies, L. E. (2016) 'A wider role for sport: Community sports hubs and urban regeneration' *Sport in Society, 19* (10): 1537–1555.

De Bosscher, V., Shibil, S., Westerbeek, H., & Van Bottenburg, M. (2015) *Successful elite sport policies: An international comparison of the Sports Policy Factors Leading to International Sporting Success (SPLISS 2.0) in 15 nations.* Aachen: Meyer & Meyer Verlag.

Dees, W. (2011) 'New media and technology use in corporate sport sponsorship: Performing activational leverage from an exchange perspective', *International Journal of Sport Management and Marketing, 10* (3–4): 272–285.

de Lissovoy, N. (2008) 'The time of educational liberation in the age of empire', In de Lissovoy, N. (ed.) *Power, crisis and education for liberation: Rethinking critical pedagogy.* New York: Macmillan, pp. 9–27.

Doherty, A., & Taylor, T. (2007) 'Sport and physical recreation in the settlement of immigrant youth', *Leisure, 31*, 27–55.

Donaldson, T., & Preston, L. E. (1995) 'The stakeholder theory of the corporation: Concepts, evidence, and implications', *Academy of management Review, 20* (1): 65–91.

Dowling, F. (2011) 'Are PE teacher identities fit for postmodern schools or are they clinging to modernist notions of professionalism?' A case study of Norwegian PE teacher students' emerging professional identities', *Sport, Education and Society, 16* (2): 201–222.

Dyson, B., Gordon, B., Cowan, J., & McKenzie, A. (2016) 'External providers and their impact on primary physical education in Aotearoa/New Zealand', *Asia-Pacific Journal of Health, Sport and Physical Education, 7* (1): 3–19.

Edens, R., & Gilsinan, J. F. (2005) 'Rethinking school partnerships', *Education and Urban Society, 37* (2): 123–138.

Evans, J. (2014) 'Neoliberalism and the future for a socio-educative physical education', *Physical Education and Sport Pedagogy, 19* (5): 545–558.

Evans, J., & Davies, B. (2014) 'Physical Education PLC: Neoliberalism, curriculum and governance. New directions for PESP research', *Sport, Education and Society, 19* (7): 869–884.

Evans, J., & Davies, B. (2015) 'Neoliberal freedoms, privatisation and the future of physical education', *Sport, Education and Society, 20* (1): 10–26.

Farahmandpur, R. (2006) 'A critical pedagogy of hope in times of despair: Teaching against global capitalism and the new imperialism', *Social Change, 36* (3): 77–91.

Ferkins, L., & Shilbury, D. (2015) 'The stakeholder dilemma in sport governance: Toward the notion of "stakeowner"', *Journal of Sport Management, 29* (1): 93–108.

Fernandez-Balboa, J. M. (1993). Sociocultural characteristics of the hidden curriculum in physical education. *Quest, 45* (2): 230–254.

FIFA (2005) Make the world a better place. http://www.fifa.com/mm/document/afprograms/worldwideprograms/fifa_ffh_en_1851.pdf

FIFA (2014) Report: Football for hope festival, Caju – Rio de Janeiro https://img.fifa.com/image/upload/e2n2xcqryofaprkdskdl.pdf

FIFA (2017) *FIFA celebrates International Day of Sport for Development and Peace.* http://www.fifa.com/sustainability/news/y=2017/m=4/news=fifa-celebrates-international-day-of-sport-for-development-and-peace-2878446.html

FIFA (2018) *Football for hope.* http://www.fifa.com/sustainability/football-for-hope.html

Ford, D. R. (2016) *Education and the production of space: Political pedagogy, geography, and urban revolution.* New York: Routledge.

Freeman, R. E., Harrison, J. S., Wicks, A. C., Parmar, B. L., & De Colle, S. (2010) *Stakeholder theory: The state of the art.* Cambridge: Cambridge University Press.

Friedman, A. L., & Miles, S. (2002) 'Developing stakeholder theory', *Journal of Management Studies, 39* (1): 1–21.

Friedman, M. T., Parent, M. M., & Mason, D. S. (2004) 'Building a framework for issues management in sport through stakeholder theory', *European Sport Management Quarterly, 4* (3): 170–190.

Freire, P. (1992) *Pedagogy of hope: Reliving the pedagogy of the oppressed.* New York: Continuum.

Freire, P. (1994/2014 [Barr, R. R., trans.]) *Reliving pedagogy of the oppressed.* New York: Bloomsbury.

Freire, P. (2000) *Pedagogy of the oppressed.* New York: Continuum.

Freire, P. (2001) *Pedagogy of freedom: Ethics, democracy and civic courage.* Lanham, MD: Rowman & Littlefield.

Freire, P. (2007) *Daring to dream: Toward a pedagogy of the unfinished.* Oxon: Routledge.

Freire, P. (2016) *Pedagogy of indignation.* Oxon: Routledge.

Frisby, W., Kikulis, L. M., & Thibault, L. (2004) 'Partnerships between local government sport and leisure departments and the commercial sector: Changes, complexities and consequences', In Slack, T. (ed.) *The commercialisation of sport.* London: Routledge, pp. 144–165.

Gaffney, C. T. (2008) *Temples of the earthbound god: Stadiums in the cultural landscapes of Rio de Janeiro and Buenos Aires.* Austin: University of Texas Press.

Gard, M. (2015) "They know they're getting the best knowledge possible': Locating the academic in changing knowledge economies', *Sport, Education & Society, 20* (1): 107–121.

Gard, M., & Wright, J. (2005) *The obesity epidemic: Science, morality and ideology.* London: Routledge.

Gates Foundation (2018) 'The 10 toughest questions we get asked', February 13, 2018, https://www.gatesnotes.com/2018-Annual-Letter?WT.mc_id=02_13_2018_02_AnnualLetter2018_DO-COM_&WT.tsrc=DOCOM

Gertner, D., & Rifkin, L. (2018) 'Coca-Cola and the fight against the global obesity epidemic', *Thunderbird International Business Review, 60* (2): 161–173.

Gibbert, M., & Ruigrok, W. (2010) 'The "what" and "how" of case study rigor: Three strategies based on published work', *Organizational Research Methods, 13* (4): 710–737.

Giroux, H. (2003) 'Dystopian nightmares and educated hopes: The return of the pedagogical and the promise of democracy', *Policy Futures in Education, 1* (3): 467–487.

Giroux, H. (2004) *The terror of neoliberalism: Authoritarianism and the eclipse of democracy.* Boulder, CO & London: Paradigm.

Giroux, H. (2007) 'Utopian thinking in dangerous times: Critical pedagogy and the project of educated hope', In Coté, M., Day, R. & de Peuter, G. (eds.) *Utopian pedagogy: Radical experiments against neoliberal globalization.* Toronto: University of Toronto Press, pp.314–324.

Giroux, H. (2009) 'Neoliberalism as public pedagogy', In Sandlin, J., Schultz, B. & Burdick, J. (eds.) *Handbook of public pedagogy: Education and learning beyond schooling.* London & New York: Routledge, pp. 486–499.

Giroux, H. A. (2005) *Schooling and the struggle for public life: Democracy's promise and education's challenge* (2nd ed.). Oxon: Routledge.

Giroux, H. A. (2011) *On critical pedagogy*. New York: Continuum.

Giroux, H. A. (2015) *University in chains: Confronting the military-industrial-academic complex*. New York: Routledge.

Giroux, H. A. (2016) *Stealing innocence: Corporate culture's war on children*. New York: Palgrave.

Giroux, H. A. (2017) 'Pedagogy, civil rights and the project of insurrectional democracy', *Howard Journal of Communications, 28* (2): 203–206.

Giulianotti, R. (2011) 'Sport, transnational peacemaking, and global civil society: Exploring the reflective discourses of "sport, development, and peace" project officials', *Journal of Sport and Social Issues, 35* (1): 50–71.

Giulianotti, R. (2015). 'Corporate social responsibility in sport: Critical issues and future possibilities', *Corporate Governance, 15* (2): 243–248.

Giulianotti, R., & Armstrong, G. (2011) Sport, the military and peacemaking: History and possibilities. *Third World Quarterly, 32* (3): 379–394.

Gleseking, J. J., Mangold, M., Katz, C., Low, S., & Saegert, S. (eds.). (2014) *The people, place, and space reader*. New York: Routledge.

Golin, J., & Campbell, M. (2017) *Reining in the commercialization of childhood. In EarthEd: Rethinking education in a changing planet*. Washington, DC: Island Press, pp. 155–164.

Goodwin, A., Snelgrove, R., Wood, L., & Taks, M. (2017) 'Leveraging charity sport events to develop a connection to a cause', *Event Management, 21* (2): 175–184.

Goodwin, M., & Grix, J. (2011) 'Bringing structures back in: The 'governance narrative', the 'decentred approach' and 'asymmetrical network governance' in the education and sport policy communities', *Public Administration, 89* (2): 537–556.

Gore, C. (2013) 'The new development cooperation landscape: Actors, approaches, architecture', *Journal of International Development, 25* (6): 769–786.

Green, M. (2009) 'Podium or participation? Analysing policy priorities under changing models of sport governance in the United Kingdom', *International Journal of Sport Policy and Politics, 1* (1): 121–144.

Green, K., & Smith, A. (eds.). (2016) *Routledge handbook of youth sport*. New York: Routledge.

Greenwood, M., & Van Buren III, H. J. (2010) 'Trust and stakeholder theory: Trustworthiness in the organisation–stakeholder relationship', *Journal of Business Ethics, 95* (3): 425–438.

Griffiths, M., & Armour, K. (2013) 'Physical education and youth sport in England: Conceptual and practical foundations for an Olympic legacy?' *International Journal of Sport Policy and Politics, 5* (2): 213–227.

Gulson, K. N. (2008) ''Neoliberal spatial technologies': On the practices of educational policy change', *Critical Studies in Education, 48* (2): 179–195.

Hackworth, J. (2007) *The neoliberal city: Governance, ideology, and development in American urbanism*. Ithaca, NY: Cornell University Press.

Harman, S. (2016) 'The Bill and Melinda Gates Foundation and legitimacy in global health governance', *Global Governance, 22,* 349–368.

Harris, S., & Houlihan, B. (2016) 'Implementing the community sport legacy: The limits of partnerships, contracts and performance management', *European Sport Management Quarterly, 16* (4): 433–458.

Harvey, S., Kirk, D., & O'Donovan, T. M. (2014) 'Sport education as a pedagogical application for ethical development in physical education and youth sport', *Sport, Education and Society, 19* (1): 41–62.

Hartmann, D., & Kwauk, C. (2011) 'Sport and development: An overview, critique, and reconstruction', *Journal of Sport and Social Issues, 35* (3): 284–305.

Hayhurst, L., Kay, T., & Chawansky, M. (2016) *Beyond sport for development and peace: Transnational perspective on theory, policy and practice.* New York: Routledge.

Hayhurst, L. M. (2011) 'Corporatising sport, gender and development: Postcolonial IR feminisms, transnational private governance and global corporate social engagement', *Third World Quarterly, 32* (3): 531–549.

Hayhurst, L. M., Wilson, B., & Frisby, W. (2011) 'Navigating neoliberal networks: Transnational internet platforms in sport for development and peace', *International Review for the Sociology of Sport, 46* (3): 315–329.

Held, V. (2006) *The ethics of care: Personal, political and global.* Oxford: Oxford University Press.

Hohenthal, J., Johanson, J., & Johanson, M. (2014) 'Network knowledge and business-relationship value in the foreign market', *International Business Review, 23* (1): 4–19.

Holt, N. L. (ed.). (2016) *Positive youth development through sport* (2nd ed.). Oxon: Routledge.

Horine, L., & Stotlar, D. (2004) *Administration of physical education and sport programs* (5th ed.). Long Grove, IL: Waveland Press.

Houlihan, B. (2014) *The government and politics of sport (RLE sports studies)* (Vol. 6). London: Routledge

Houlihan, B. (2016) *Sport policy making. Routledge handbook of sport and politics.* New York: Routledge

Houlihan, B., & Bradbury, S. (2013) *10 years of teamwork: McDonald's national grassroots football partnership 2002–2012: Coaching the coaches, valuing the volunteers and growing the game: Executive summary.* London: McDonalds.

Houlihan, B., & Lindsey, I. (2012) *Sport policy in Britain* (Vol. 18). London: Routledge.

International Olympic Committee (2017) *Olympic charter.* Lausanne: International Olympic Committee.

Jane, B., & Gibson, K. (2017) 'Corporate sponsorship of physical activity promotion programmes: Part of the solution or part of the problem?' *Journal of Public Health, 40*: 1–10.

Jansson, D., & Koch, N. (2017) 'Toward a critical geography of sport: Space, power, and social justice', In Koch, N. (ed.) *Critical geographies of sport: Space, power and sport in global perspective,* London: Routledge, pp. 237–252.

Jenkins, H., & James, L. (2012) *It's not just a game: Community work in the UK football industry and approaches to corporate social responsibility*. Cardiff: The ESRC Centre for Business Relationship, Accountability, Sustainability and Society, Cardiff University

Jensen, M. C. (2010) 'Value maximization, stakeholder theory, and the corporate objective function', *Journal of Applied Corporate Finance, 22* (1): 32–42.

Jones, M., Jones, R., Woods, M., Whitehead, M., Dixon, D., & Hannah, M. (2014) *An introduction to political geography: Space, place and politics*. Oxon: Routledge.

Jules, T. D. (2017). "'Mature regionalism' and the genesis of 'functional projects': 'educational regionalism' in small (and micro-states)', *Globalisation, Societies and Education, 15* (4): 482–498.

Kaul, I. (2006) 'Exploring the policy space between markets and states', In Kaul, I. & Conceicao, P. (eds.) *The new public finance: Responding to global challenges*, Oxford: Oxford University Press, pp. 219–268.

Kay, T., & Dudfield, O. (2013) *The commonwealth guide to advancing development through sport*. London: Commonwealth Secretariat.

Kincheloe, J. L. (2002) *The sign of the Burger: McDonald's and the culture of power*. Philadelphia, PA: Temple University Press.

Kincheloe, J. L. (2008a) *Knowledge and critical pedagogy: An introduction*. New York: Springer.

Kincheloe, J. L. (2008b) *Critical pedagogy* (2nd ed.). New York: Peter Lang.

Kivisto, H. (2016) 'Capital as power and the corporatisation of education', *Critical Studies in Education*, 1–17. doi:10.1080/17508487.2016.1186707.

Knight, G. (2007) 'Activism, risk and communicational politics: Nike and the sweatshop problem', In May, S., Cheney, G., & Roper, J. (eds.) *The debate over corporate social responsibility*, Oxford: Oxford University, pp. 305–318.

Knoke, D. (2018) *Changing organizations: Business networks in the new political economy*. New York: Routledge.

Koggel, C. (1998) *Perspectives on equality: Constructing a relational theory*. Lanham, MD: Rowman & Littlefield.

Koggel, C., & Orme, J. (2010) 'Care ethics: New theories and applications', *Ethics and Social Welfare, 4* (2): 109–114.

Kohe, G., & Newman, J. (2011) 'Body commons: Toward an interdisciplinary study of the somatic spectacular', *Brogla: An Australian Journal about Dance, 35* (December): 65–74.

Kohe, G. Z. (2010) 'Disrupting the rhetoric of the rings: A critique of Olympic idealism in physical education', *Sport, Education and Society, 15* (4): 479–494.

Kohe, G. Z. (2015) 'Still playing together(?): A recall to physical education and sport history intersections', *The International Journal of the History of Sport, 32* (15): 1745–1749.

Kohe, G. Z., & Chatziefstathiou, D. (2017) 'Olympic education in the United Kingdom: Rethinking London 2012 learning 'legacies' and their pedagogical potential', In Naul, R., Binder, D., Rychtecky, A., & Culpan, I. (eds.) *Olympic education: An international review*. London: Routledge, pp. 60–72.

Kohe, G. Z., & Collison, H. (2019) 'Playing on common ground: Spaces of sport, education and corporate connectivity, contestation and creativity', *Sport in Society*. doi: 10.1080/17430437.2018.1555219.

Kombe, C. L. M., & Herman, C. (2017) 'Can educational innovations be sustained after the end of donor funding? The case of a reading educational programme in Zambia', *Educational Review, 69* (5): 533–553.

Kornum, N., Gyrd-Jones, R., Al Zagir, N., & Brandis, K. A. (2017) 'Interplay between intended brand identity and identities in a Nike related brand community: Co-existing synergies and tensions in a nested system', *Journal of Business Research, 70*, 432–440.

Korschun, D., Bhattacharya, C. B., & Swain, S. D. (2014). Corporate social responsibility, customer orientation, and the job performance of frontline employees. *Journal of Marketing, 78* (3): 20–37.

Lavalette, M. (ed.). (2013) *Capitalism and sport: Politics, protest, people and play*. London: Bookmarks.

Lawn Tennis Association (2013) 'British Tennis welcomes government funding for school sport'. https://www3.lta.org.uk/Tennis-Foundation/News1/2013/Latest-News---March/British-tennis-welcomes-Government-funding-for-school-sport/, accessed 12 June 2018.

Lee, A., & Lambert, C. (2017) 'Corporate social responsibility in McDonald's Australia', *Asian Case Research Journal, 21* (2): 393–430.

Lefebvre, H. (1991a [Nicholson-Smith, D., trans.]) *The production of space*. Oxford: Blackwell.

Lefebvre, H. (1991b [Moore, J., trans.]) *The critique of everyday life* (Vol. 1.). London: Verso.

Lefebvre, H. (1996 [Kofman, E. & Lebas, E., trans & eds.]) *Writings on cities*. Oxford: Blackwell.

Lefebvre, H. (2003 [Elden, S., Lebas, E., & Kofman, E., eds.]) *Key writings*. Oxford: Blackwell.

Lefebvre, H., & Réguiler, C. (1986/2004 [Elden, S. & Moore, G. trans]) *Rhythmanalysis: Space, time and everyday life*. London: Continuum, pp. 87–100.

Lenskyj, H. J. (2012) 'Olympic education and Olympism: Still colonizing young people's minds', *Educational Review, 64* (3): 265–274.

Levermore, R. (2010) 'CSR for development through sport: Examining its potential and limitations', *Third World Quarterly, 31* (2): 223–241.

Levermore, R., & Beacom, A. (eds.). (2009) *Sport and international development*. New York: Palgrave.

Levermore, R., & Moore, N. (2015) 'The need to apply new theories to "Sport CSR"', *Corporate Governance, 15* (2): 249–253.

Lewis, T. (2006) 'Utopia and education in critical theory', *Policy Futures in Education, 4* (1): 6–17.

Lindsey, I. (2013) 'Community collaboration in development work with young people: Perspectives from Zambian communities', *Development in Practice, 23* (4): 481–495.

Lindsey, I., & Grattan, A. (2012) 'An 'international movement'? Decentring sport-for-development within Zambian communities', *International Journal of Sport Policy and Politics, 4* (1): 91–110.

Lindsey, I., Kay, T., Jeanes, R., & Banda, D. (2017) *Localizing global sport for development.* Manchester: Manchester University Press.

Lipman, P. (2015) 'Capitalizing on crisis: Venture philanthropy's colonial project to remake urban education', *Critical Studies in Education, 56* (2): 241–258.

Macdonald, D. (2011) 'Like a fish in water: PE policy and practice in the era of neoliberal globalization', *Quest, 63* (1): 36–45.

Macdonald, D. (2014) 'Is global neo-liberalism shaping the future of physical education?' *Physical Education and Sport Pedagogy, 19* (5): 494–499.

Macdonald, D. (2015) 'Teacher-as-knowledge-broker in a futures oriented health and physical education', *Sport, Education and Society, 20* (1): 27–41.

Macdonald, D., Hay, P., & Williams, B. (2008) 'Should you buy? Neo-liberalism, neo-HPE, and your neo-job', *New Zealand Physical Educator, 41*, 6–13.

Mac Ginty, R., & Richmond, O. P. (2013) 'The local turn in peace building: A critical agenda for peace', *Third World Quarterly, 34* (5): 763–783.

Mahdi, H. A. A., Abbas, M., Mazar, T. I., & George, S. (2015) 'A comparative analysis of strategies and business models of Nike, Inc. and Adidas Group with special reference to competitive advantage in the context of a dynamic and competitive environment', *International Journal of Business Management and Economic Research, 6* (3): 167–177.

Maguire, J. A. (2011) 'Power and global sport: Zones of prestige, emulation and resistance', *Sport in Society, 14* (7–8): 1010–1026.

Malaw, H., & Marcesseault, D. (2016) 'Finding the missing voices of Sport for Development and Peace (SDP): Using a 'Participatory Social Interaction Research' methodology and anthropological perspective within African developing countries', *Sport in Society, 21* (2): 226–242.

Malcolm, D. (2012) *Globalizing cricket: Englishness, empire and identity.* London: Bloomsbury.

Mansfield, L. (2014) 'Towards an understanding of netball in Malawi, international sport development and identification: Theoretical and methodological sensitizing issues', *Sport in Society, 17* (4): 492–506.

Marcuse, H. (1968) 'Lecture on education, Brooklyn College', In Kellner, D., Lewis, T., Pierce, C., & Cho, D. (eds.) *Marcuse's challenge to education.* New York: Rowman & Littlefield, pp. 33–38.

Marcuse, H. (1975) 'Lecture on higher education and politics, Berkeley', In D. Kellner, D., Lewis, T., Pierce, C., & Cho, D. (eds.) *Marcuse's challenge to education.* New York: Rowman & Littlefield, pp. 39–44.

Marsh, V. (2017) 'The war on childhood: Commercialism in schools and the first amendment', *Houston Law Review, 55*, 511.

Martin, A., Morgan, S., Parnell, D., Philpott, M., Pringle, A., Rigby, M., ... Topham, J. (2016) 'A perspective from key stakeholders on football and health improvement', *Soccer & Society, 17* (2): 175–182.

McCartney, M. (2014) 'Is Coca-Cola's anti-obesity scheme the real thing?' *British Medical Journal, 349*, 4340.

McCoy, D. (2011) 'Global health and the Gates Foundation', In Rushton, S. & Williams, O. D. (eds.) *Partnerships and foundations in global health governance.* London: Palgrave Macmillan, pp. 143–163.

McEwan, C., & Goodman, M. K. (2010) 'Place geography and the ethics of care: Introductory remarks on the geographies of ethics, responsibility and care', *Ethics, Place and Environment, 13* (2): 103–112.

McGoey, L. (2015) *No such thing as a free gift: The Gates Foundation and the price of philanthropy.* London: Verso Books.

McKeown-Moak, M. P. (2013) 'The "new" performance funding for higher education', *Educational Considerations, 40* (2): 3–12.

McLaren, P., & Sandlin, J. A. (2010) 'Teaching against consumer capitalism in the age of commercialization and corporatization of public education', In Sandlin, J. A. & McLaren, P. (eds.) *Critical pedagogies of consumption.* London: Routledge, pp. 84–92.

Meier, C. (2017) 'The early relationship between UNESCO and the IOC: Considerations–Controversies–Cooperation', *Diagoras: International Academic Journal on Olympic Studies, 1*, 229–248.

Merk, J. (2015) 'Global outsourcing and socialisation of labour–The case of Nike', In van der Pil, K. (ed.) *The International Political Economy of Production.* Cheltenham: Edward Elgar, pp. 115–131.

Miles, S. (2012) 'Stakeholder: Essentially contested or just confused?' *Journal of Business Ethics, 108* (3): 285–298.

Miles, S. (2017) 'Stakeholder theory classification: A theoretical and empirical evaluation of definitions', *Journal of Business Ethics, 142* (3): 437–459.

Mills, L. (2010) 'The corporatization of women's football in South Africa: A case study of the Sasol sponsorship and its transformative potential', In Shehu, J. (ed.) *Gender, sport and development in Africa: Cross cultural perspectives on patterns of representations and marginalization.* Dakar: CODESRIA, pp. 125–134.

Mitchell, K. (2001) 'Transnationalism, neo-liberalism, and the rise of the shadow state', *Economy and Society, 30*, 165–189.

Molnar, A. (2005) *School commercialism: From democratic ideal to market commodity.* New York: Routledge.

Molnar, A., & Boninger, F. (2015) *Sold out: How marketing in school threatens children's well-being and undermines their education.* New York: Rowman & Littlefield.

Moran, A. J., Rimm, E. B., & Taveras, E. M. (2017) 'A school-based brand marketing program's adherence to federal nutrition criteria', *American Journal of Preventive Medicine, 53* (5): 710–713.

Morran, C. (2016) 'Teachers call on McDonald's to end McTeacher's Nights', Consumerist. Retrieved 19 August 2017. https://www.corporatecrimereporter.com/news/200/teachers-challenge-mcdonalds-over-mcteachers-night/

Müller, M. (2015) 'Assemblages and actor-networks: Rethinking socio-material power, politics and space', *Geography Compass, 9* (1): 27–41.

Mwaanga, O., & Mwansa, K. (2013) 'Indigenous discourses in sport for development and peace: A case study of the Ubuntu cultural philosophy in EduSport Foundation, Zambia', In Schulenkorf, N. & Adair, D. (eds.) *Global sport-for-development*. London: Palgrave Macmillan, pp. 115–133.

Naul, R., Binder, D., Rychtecky, A., & Culpan, I. (eds.). (2017) *Olympic education: An international review*. New York: Routledge.

Neesham, G., & Garnham, A. P. (2012) 'Success story: Clontarf Foundation promotes education, life-skills and employment prospects through Australian Rules Football', *British Journal of Sports Medicine, 146*, 898–899.

Nenonen, S., & Storbacka, K. (2010) 'Business model design: Conceptualizing networked value co-creation', *International Journal of Quality and Service Sciences, 2* (1): 43–59.

Nicholls, S., Giles, A. R., & Sethna, C. (2011) 'Perpetuating the 'lack of evidence' discourse in sport for development: Privileged voices, unheard stories and subjugated knowledge', *International Review for the Sociology of Sport, 46* (3): 249–264.

Nichols Jr, J. R. (2016) 'The economic citizen: Civic education and its discontents', In Nichols Jr, J. R. (eds.) *Teaching for democracy in an age of economic disparity*. Oxon: Routledge, pp. 33–49.

Nike Inc., American College of Sports Medicine & International Council of Sport Science and Physical Education (eds.) (2013) *'Designed to move' Report*. http://e13c7a4144957cea5013-f2f5ab26d5e83af3ea377013dd602911.r77.cf5.rackcdn.com/resources/pdf/en/full-report.pdf, accessed 3 June 2018.

Nishtar, S. (2004) Public-private 'partnerships' in health – A global call to action. *Health Research Policy Systems, 2* (1): 5. doi:10.1186/1478–4505-2–5.

Olmedo, A. (2013) 'Policy-makers, market advocates and edu-businesses: New and renewed players in the Spanish education policy arena', *Journal of Education Policy, 28* (1): 55–76.

O'Reilly, N., & Brunet, M. K. (2013) *Public-private partnerships in physical activity and sport*. Champaign, IL: Human Kinetics.

Oruc, I., & Sarikaya, M. (2011) Normative stakeholder theory in relation to ethics of care. *Social Responsibility Journal, 7* (3): 381–392.

Peachey, J. W., Zhou, Y., Damon, Z. J., & Burton, L. J. (2015) Forty years of leadership research in sport management: A review, synthesis, and conceptual framework. *Journal of Sport Management, 29* (5): 570–587.

Peck, J., & Tickell, A. (2002) 'Neoliberalizing space', In Brenner, N. & Theodore, N. (eds.) *Spaces of neoliberalism: Urban restructuring in North America and Western Europe*. Oxford: Blackwell, pp. 33–57.

Penney, D., Petrie, K., & Fellows, S. (2015) 'HPE in Aotearoa New Zealand: The reconfiguration of policy and pedagogic relations and privatisation of curriculum and pedagogy', *Sport, Education and Society, 20* (1): 42–56.

Petrie, K., Penney, D., & Fellows, S. (2014) 'Health and physical education in Aotearoa New Zealand: An open market and open doors?' *Asia-Pacific Journal of Health, Sport and Physical Education, 5* (1): 19–38.

Pettersen, T. (2011) 'The ethics of care: Normative structures and empirical implications', *Health Care Analysis, 19* (1): 51–64.

Picciano, A., & Spring, J. (2012) *The great American education-industrial complex: Ideology, technology, and profit.* New York: Routledge.

Piggin, J. (2015) 'Designed to move? Physical activity lobbying and the politics of productivity', *Health Education Journal, 74* (1): 16–27.

Powell, D. (2015) 'Assembling the privatisation of physical education the 'in-expert' teacher', *Sport, Education & Society, 20* (1): 73–88.

Powell, D. (2018). The 'will to give': Corporations, philanthropy and schools. *Journal of Education Policy,* 1–20. doi:10.1080/02680939.2018.1424940.

Powell, D., & Gard, M. (2015) 'The governmentality of childhood obesity: Coca-Cola, public health and primary schools', *Discourse: Studies in the Cultural Politics of Education, 36* (6): 854–867.

Press, F., & Woodrow, C. (2005) 'Commodification, corporatisation and children's spaces', *Australian Journal of Education, 49* (3): 278–291.

Pretty, J., Peacock, J., Sellens, M., & Griffin, M. (2005) 'The mental and physical health outcomes of green exercise', *International Journal of Environmental Health Research, 15* (5): 319–337.

Preuss, H. (2015) A framework for identifying the legacies of a mega sport event. *Leisure Studies, 34* (6): 643–664.

Reckhow, S., & Snyder, J. W. (2014) 'The expanding role of philanthropy in education politics', *Educational Researcher, 43* (4): 186–195.

Renold, E. (1997). "All they've got on their brains is football'. Sport, masculinity and the gendered practices of playground relations', *Sport, Education and Society, 2* (1): 5–23.

Robinson, D. B., Gleddie, D., & Schaefer, L. (2016) 'Telling and selling: A consideration of the pedagogical work done by nationally endorsed corporate-sponsored educational resources', *Asia-Pacific Journal of Health, Sport and Physical Education, 7* (1): 37–54.

Rossi, T., & Jeanes, R. (2016) 'Education, pedagogy and sport for development: Addressing seldom asked questions', *Sport, Education and Society, 21* (4): 483–494.

Rowe, K., Karg, A., & Sherry, E. (2018) 'Community-orientated practice: Examining corporate social responsibility and development activities in professional sport', *Sport Management Review.* doi:10.1016/j.smr.2018.05.001.

Rushton, S., & Williams, O. D. (eds.). (2011) *Partnerships and foundations in global health governance.* London: Palgrave Macmillan.

Russo, A., & Perrini, F. (2010) 'Investigating stakeholder theory and social capital: CSR in large firms and SMEs', *Journal of Business Ethics, 91* (2): 207–221.

Salcines, J. L. P., Babiak, K., & Walters, G. (eds.). (2013) *Routledge handbook of sport and corporate social responsibility.* Oxon: Routledge.

Saltman, K. (2012) 'Why Henry Giroux's democratic pedagogy is crucial for confronting failed corporate school reform and how liberals like Ravitch and Darling-Hammond are making things worse', *Policy Futures in Education, 10* (6): 674–68.

Sanders, B., Phillips, J., & Vanreusel, B. (2014) 'Opportunities and challenges facing NGOs using sport a vehicle for development in post-Apartheid South Africa', *Sport, Education & Society, 19* (6): 789–805.

Sandlin, J., Schultz, B., & Burdick, J. (eds.). (2009) *Handbook of public pedagogy: Education and learning beyond schooling.* London & New York: Routledge.

Schulenkorf, N. (2012) 'Sustainable community development through sport and events: A conceptual framework for sport-for-development projects', *Sport Management Review, 15* (1): 1–12.

Schulenkorf, N., & Edwards, D. (2012) 'Maximizing positive social impacts: Strategies for sustaining and leveraging the benefits of intercommunity sport events in divided societies', *Journal of Sport Management, 26* (5): 379–390.

Scott, J. (2009) 'The politics of venture philanthropy in charter school policy and advocacy', *Educational Policy, 23*, 106–136.

Sevenhuijsen, S. (1998) *Citizenship and the ethics of care.* London: Routledge.

SHAPE America – Society of Health and Physical Educators and Voices for Healthy Kids (2016) *SHAPE of the Nation Report.* Montgomery, AL: SHAPE.

Sheilds, R. (1999) *Lefebvre, love & struggle: Spatial dialectics.* New York: Routledge.

Sherwood, M., Nicholson, M., & Marjoribanks, T. (2017) 'Controlling the message and the medium? The impact of sports organisations' digital and social channels on media access' *Digital Journalism, 5* (5): 513–531.

Slater, G. (2015) 'Education as recovery: Neoliberalism, school reform, and the politics of crisis', *Journal of Education Policy, 30* (1): 1–20.

Smillie, I., Helmich, H., Randel, J., & German, T. (eds.). (2013) *Stakeholders: Government-NGO partnerships for international development.* New York: Routledge.

Smith, A. C., & Westerbeek, H. M. (2007) 'Sport as a vehicle for deploying corporate social responsibility', *Journal of Corporate Citizenship, 25* (1): 43–54.

Sotiriadou, K. (2009) 'The Australian sport system and its stakeholders: Development of cooperative relationships', *Sport in Society, 12* (7): 842–860.

Spaaij, R. (2012) 'Building social and cultural capital among young people in disadvantaged communities: Lessons from a Brazilian sport-based intervention program', *Sport, Education and Society, 17* (1): 77–95.

Stenling, C., & Fahlén, J. (2016) 'Same same, but different? Exploring the organizational identities of Swedish voluntary sports: Possible implications of sports clubs' self-identification for their role as implementers of policy objectives', *International Review for the Sociology of Sport, 51* (7): 867–883.

Studdert, D., & Walkerdine, V. (2016) 'Space, geography and social power', In Studdert, D. & Walkerdine, V. (eds.) *Rethinking community research.* London: Palgrave Macmillan, pp. 127–160.

Svensson, P. G. (2017) 'Organizational hybridity: A conceptualization of how sport for development and peace organizations respond to divergent institutional demands', *Sport Management Review, 20* (5): 443–454.

Tantalo, C., & Priem, R. L. (2016) Value creation through stakeholder synergy. *Strategic Management Journal, 37* (2): 314–329.

The Tennis Foundation (2018) http://www.tennisfoundation.org.uk/

Thorne McAlister, D., & Ferrell, L. (2002) 'The role of strategic philanthropy in marketing strategy', *European Journal of Marketing, 36* (5/6): 689–705.

Thorpe, H., Hayhurst, L. M., & Chawansky, M. (2018) 'The girl effect and "positive" representations of sporting girls of the Global South: Social media portrayals of Afghan girls on skateboards', In Toffoletti, K., Francombe-Webb, J., & Thorpe, H. (eds.) *New sporting femininities.* Cham: Palgrave Macmillan, pp. 299–323.

Toppinen, A., & Korhonen-Kurki, K. (2013) 'Global reporting initiative and social impact in managing corporate responsibility: A case study of three multinationals in the forest industry', *Business Ethics: A European Review, 22* (2): 202–217.

Torres, A. (2008) *Education and neoliberal globalization.* London & New York: Routledge.

Tronto, J. (1993) *Moral boundaries: A political argument for an ethic of care.* London: Routledge.

Tuan, Y. F. (1977) *Space and place: The perspective of experience.* Minneapolis: University of Minnesota Press.

UK Active (2017) *Park lives report.* London: UK Active, http://researchinstitute.ukactive.com/downloads/managed/CocaColaParkLives_Year3Evaluation-Report_Final.pdf

UNESCO (2015). *Education 2030 Incheon declaration and framework for action.* New York: UNESCO. http://unesdoc.unesco.org/images/0024/002456/245656E.pdf

UNGA (United Nations General Assembly) (2007) *Resolution adopted by the General Assembly. The Rights of the Child.* New York: United Nations A/RES/62/141.

UNICEF (2015) *Progress for children: Child protection.* New York: UNICEF.

UNICEF (2017) *Humanitarian action for children.* New York: UNICEF.

United Nations (2015) *Transforming our world: The 2030 agenda for sustainable development.* New York: United Nations.

Vance, L., Raciti, M. M., & Lawley, M. (2016) 'Sponsorship selections: Corporate culture, beliefs and motivations', *Corporate Communications: An International Journal, 21* (4): 483–499.

Van den Hurk, M., & Verhoest, K. (2015) 'The governance of public–private partnerships in sports infrastructure: Interfering complexities in Belgium', *International Journal of Project Management, 33* (1): 201–211.

van der Roest, J. W., Spaaij, R., & van Bottenburg, M. (2015) 'Mixed methods in emerging academic subdisciplines: The case of sport management', *Journal of Mixed Methods Research, 9* (1): 70–90.

Van Ingen, C. (2003) 'Geographies of gender, sexuality and race: Reframing the focus on space in sport sociology', *International Review for the Sociology of Sport, 38* (2): 201–216.

Wagner Mainardes, E., Alves, H., & Raposo, M. (2011) 'Stakeholder theory: Issues to resolve', *Management Decision, 49* (2): 226–252.

Walker, C. M., & Hayton, J. W. (2018) 'An analysis of third sector sport organisations in an era of 'super-austerity'', *International Journal of Sport Policy and Politics, 10* (1): 43–61.

Walters, G., & Chadwick, S. (2009) 'Corporate citizenship in football: Delivering strategic benefits through stakeholder engagement', *Management Decision, 47* (1): 51–66.

Wasser, K., & Misener, L. (2016) 'International sport development', In Sherry, E., Schulenkork, N & Phillips, P. (eds.) *Managing sport development.* Oxon: Routledge, pp. 31–44.

Weed, M., Coren, E., Fiore, J., Wellard, I., Chatziefstathiou, D., Mansfield, L., & Dowse, S. (2015) 'The Olympic Games and raising sport participation: A systematic review of evidence and an interrogation of policy for a demonstration effect', *European Sport Management Quarterly, 15* (2): 195–226.

Werther, Jr, W. B., & Chandler, D. (2010) *Strategic corporate social responsibility: Stakeholders in a global environment.* London: Sage.

Westerbeek, H., & Smith, A. (2005) *Business leadership and lessons from sport.* New York: Springer.

Whitley, M. A., Coble, C., & Jewell, G. S. (2016) 'Evaluation of a sport-based youth development programme for refugees', *Leisure/Loisir, 40* (2): 175–199.

Whipp, P. R., Hutton, H., Grove, J. R., & Jackson, B. (2011) 'Outsourcing Physical Education in primary schools: Evaluating the impact of externally provided programmes on generalist teachers', *Asia-Pacific Journal of Health, Sport & Physical Education, 2* (2): 67–77.

Whitson, D. (1998) 'Circuits of promotion: Media, marketing and the globalization of sport', In Wenner, L. (ed.) *MediaSport.* London: Routledge, pp. 57–72.

Williams, B. J., & Macdonald, D. (2015) 'Explaining outsourcing in health, sport and physical education', *Sport, Education and Society, 20* (1): 57–72.

Wilson, B., & Hayhurst, L. (2009) 'Digital activism: Neoliberalism the internet, and sport for youth development', *Sociology of Sport Journal, 26* (1): 155–181.

Wright, J., & Macdonald, D. (eds.). (2010) *Young people, physical activity and the everyday.* London: Routledge.

Yancey, A., Winfield, D., Larsen, J., Anderson, M., Jackson, P., Overton, J., ... Kumanyika, S. (2009) '"Live, Learn and Play": Building strategic alliance between professional sports and public health', *Preventative Medicine, 49* (4): 322–325.

Youde, J. (2013) 'The Rockefeller and Gates Foundations in global health governance', *Global Society, 27* (2): 139–158.

Young Foundation (2012) *'Move It' report.* London: Young Foundation.

Zott, C., Amit, R., & Massa, L. (2011) The business model: Recent developments and future research. *Journal of Management, 37* (4): 1019–1042.

Index

Note: **Bold** page numbers refer to tables.